SELLING BEYOND BORDERS

PROVEN STRATEGIES TO GO GLOBAL

AMAR KHURANA

Worldwide Published by
Pendown Press

PENDOWN PRESS LLP

An ISO 9001 & ISO 14001 Certified Co.

Regd. Office 3767A, Kanhaiya Nagar,
Tri Nagar, Delhi-110035

Ph.: 8130886000, 9650072927, 8595249536

E-mail: info@pendownpress.com

Branch Office 1A/2A, 20, Hari Sadan, Ansari Road,
Daryaganj, New Delhi-110002

Ph.: 011-45794768

Website: PendownPress.com

First Edition: 2023

Price: ₹499/-

ISBN: 978-93-5554-748-4

All Rights Reserved

All the ideas and thoughts in this book are given by the author and he is responsible for the treatise, facts and dialogues used in this book. He is also responsible for the used pictures and the permission to use them in this book. Copyright of this book is reserved with the author. The publisher does not have any responsibility for the above-mentioned matters. No part of this publication may be reproduced, distributed, or transmitted in any form or by any means, including photocopying, recording, or other electronic or mechanical methods, without the prior written permission of the publisher and author.

Layout and Cover Designed by Pendown Graphics Team

Printed and Bound in India by Thomson ress India Ltd.

Contents

Strategy 5: Sales and Marketing Strategies

Strategy 6: Effective Communication and Negotiation

Strategy 7: Managing International Teams

Strategy 8: Continuous Growth and Adaptation

Preface

Welcome to the world of global selling, where borders are no longer barriers and opportunities for growth and expansion are boundless. In today's interconnected and dynamic marketplace, businesses have the chance to reach customers across the globe, tapping into new markets and unlocking tremendous potential. This book is your guide to becoming a successful global seller, navigating the complexities of international trade, and capitalizing on the vast opportunities that exist in different corners of the world. Drawing upon my wealth of expertise in the field, I have distilled my years of experience and insights into these pages, aiming to provide you with a comprehensive roadmap to achieve global success.

The journey of becoming a global seller is an exciting one, but it also comes with its fair share of challenges. From understanding intricate cultural nuances and navigating dynamic market forces to developing effective strategies for localization and overcoming logistical hurdles, there are many facets to consider. This book is your trusted resource, arming you with knowledge, strategies, and tools to navigate these challenges and emerge as a global leader.

Throughout the upcoming chapters, we'll cover lots of important stuff to help you succeed as a global seller. We'll talk about the good and tough parts of selling globally, and why it's important to embrace change and try new things.

We'll dig into doing thorough research on the market and coming up with smart ways to beat your competition and make your brand stand out. You'll also learn how to understand what customers want, adapt your products, and create a great brand story that appeals to people all over the world. Plus, we'll dive into using digital tools, handling shipping and partners, and making sure you have the right amount of stuff in stock.

Furthermore, this book will guide you in creating a smart global sales plan, tailoring your ads to connect with different customers, using social media influencers and partners to reach more people, and getting really good at talking to people from different cultures, even if you don't speak the same language. As we go along, we'll stress how important it is to build trust and keep good relationships with people from other countries who are part of your business. We'll also look at why having a diverse team is great and how to work well together, even if you're far away from each other.

In today's fast-changing global market, it's super important to keep up with what's happening. This book will show you how to do that and adjust your plans. Plus, it'll teach you how to make money in different ways and use new technology to do well. Each part of the book has practical tips and real examples that you can use right away. Whether you're a pro at business looking to go global or just starting out and dreaming big, this book will help you. Remember, the road to global success can be bumpy, but with the right thinking, knowledge, and plans, you can get past problems and grab great opportunities. So, let's go on this journey together and explore the world as our marketplace, finding all the awesome chances waiting for us.

Wishing you a fruitful and fulfilling journey as a global seller.

~Amar Khurana

Foreword

In the vast world of business, there are exceptional individuals who shine not just for what they achieve but also for their positive energy and never-give-up attitude. Amardeep Singh Khurana, the founder of Inext Group of Companies and House of Brands Canada, is one such extraordinary person. As a true Virgo, he's all about happiness, optimism, and always chasing success.

Amardeep Singh Khurana's illustrious 22-year career spans regulatory expertise, supply chain and logistics proficiency, and serial entrepreneurship. His fervent commitment to logistics and supply chain solutions culminated in the establishment of Inext Logistic Group, now a premier global supply chain service provider and the fastest-growing integrated logistics enterprise in Asia. With its headquarters in New Delhi, India, Inext Logistics has cultivated a formidable presence worldwide, thanks to a dedicated network of partners. Under Amardeep's astute leadership, Inext Logistics has transitioned from a customs brokerage firm into a major logistics player, boasting offices in Canada, India, Hong Kong, and China. The company has earned trust as a preferred partner for renowned brands in India and beyond, a testament to Amardeep's unwavering commitment to industry expertise and operational excellence.

Amardeep Singh Khurana's recent launch of House of Brands Canada goes beyond his remarkable accomplishments, exemplifying his entrepreneurial drive, keen eye for new opportunities, and commitment to bridging cultural and market divides. This pioneering venture not only provides a platform for promoting Indian businesses in North America but also symbolizes Amardeep's dedication to fostering growth, collaboration, and cross-cultural exchange on the international stage. Beyond his business acumen, Amardeep inspires everyone he encounters with his infectious optimism, infusing a unique vitality into all his endeavors. He serves as a compelling reminder that success encompasses not just financial gain but also finding joy and purpose in our work while positively impacting the lives of others.

Amardeep Singh Khurana, a hardworking Virgo, balances his strong sense of responsibility with a joyful spirit. He's succeeded in business by paying attention to details. He also knows how to enjoy life. In addition to his business achievements, he's an author with two upcoming books. In these books, he shares his wisdom and experiences to inspire and teach aspiring entrepreneurs and anyone interested in international business, bringing the same dedication and joy that define his approach to life, both in and out of the business world.

As we wrap up, I'm thrilled to present this book, which showcases the wisdom and forward-thinking of Amardeep Singh Khurana. Inside, you'll go on a journey guided by a real industry expert. Amardeep's story reminds us that passion, adaptability, and self-belief can take you anywhere in the world of success.

Now, let's jump into the upcoming pages, packed with smart ideas, useful tips, and stories that inspire. Let's catch the spirit of Amardeep Singh Khurana, the real go-getter who loves life, just like a true Virgo.

Together, let us discover the boundless possibilities that await us in the world of global business.

Acknowledgements

I want to say a big thank you to all the people who helped make "Selling Beyond Borders" a reality. Your support and belief in me have been amazing.

My Gurus and mentors: Rahul Jain, Akshar Yadav, Ravi Kapoor, Jagmohan Singh, Sanjeev Jain, and Vivek Bindra, you all have been like wise teachers, showing me the path to success. I truly value your guidance.

My Parents: You've always been my strength, teaching me the values of hard work and not giving up. Your love and encouragement made me who I am today.

My Wife, Meghana: You've been there for me all along this writing journey, and your belief in me is what this book is built on.

My Two Beautiful Daughters, Kashvi and Aashvi: You're the reason I do everything I do. Your love and innocence remind me every day to keep trying new things.

My Team at Inext Group: You've worked really hard, and our success is because of your dedication. I'm proud to have such a great team.

My Customers: You've trusted us and stayed with us, helping our business move forward. Your feedback and support mean a lot.

Well-Wishers: To everyone who cheered me on, thank you for believing in what I do. Your positivity kept me going.

This book wouldn't have happened without all of you. Your roles in my life and this project are huge, and I'm very thankful for you all.

With a lot of love,

Cheers to your global selling adventure! This book is like your secret weapon, packed with tips and ideas to conquer international markets. Get set to shine as a global seller!

Chapter 1

Embracing a Global Mindset: Understanding the Advantages and Challenges of Global Selling

Introduction

In today's interconnected world, businesses of all sizes have the opportunity to expand their horizons and reach customers beyond their local markets. This global reach has become increasingly accessible due to advancements in technology, logistics, and communication. However, embarking on the journey of global selling is not without its complexities and challenges. To succeed in the global marketplace, it is crucial to embrace a global mindset and thoroughly understand the advantages and challenges that come with it.

The Global Marketplace

The global marketplace is a vast and dynamic ecosystem where businesses from different countries and cultures interact and compete. This marketplace is characterized by its diversity, complexity, and ever-evolving nature. Here, companies have the chance to tap into a global customer base, explore new revenue streams, and gain a competitive edge. However, to navigate this intricate landscape successfully, it's essential to first acknowledge the advantages it offers and the challenges it presents.

Advantages of Global Selling

- **Expanded Customer Base:**

  Global selling opens doors to a much larger customer pool, potentially increasing sales and revenue.

- **Diversification of Demand:**

  Venturing into international markets taps into new sources of demand, reducing reliance on a single market and providing a buffer against economic fluctuations.

- **Stimulates Innovation:**

  Adapting to new markets often leads to product development or enhancement, driving innovation within a company.

- **Cost Efficiencies:**

  Selling in larger quantities can lead to cost savings in manufacturing, distribution, and marketing, ultimately boosting profit margins.

- **Access to Specialized Resources:**

  Global expansion provides access to skilled labor, unique technologies, or specific raw materials not readily available domestically, improving product quality and fostering innovation.

- **Risk Mitigation:**

  Establishing a presence in multiple markets reduces dependence on the economic health of one market, acting as a robust risk mitigation strategy to stabilize overall company finances during economic downturns or challenges.

Challenges of Global Selling

- **Complex Regulatory Landscape:**

  Navigating international regulations, tariffs, and trade agreements in diverse countries can be time-consuming and costly, requiring meticulous compliance efforts.

- **Cultural Differences:**

  Varied cultural norms and practices can lead to misunderstandings and reputational damage. Successful global selling demands effective communication and a deep understanding of local customs, business etiquette, and consumer preferences.

- **Language Barriers:**

  Overcoming language differences is essential for building trust and strong global business relationships, necessitating multilingual capabilities.

- **Logistical Complexities:**

  Managing supply chains across borders involves meticulous attention to transportation infrastructures, time zones, and customs procedures, adding to the complexity of global operations.

- **Currency Fluctuations:**

  Exchange rate volatility can impact pricing, profitability, and financial stability. Effective strategies for managing and hedging against these risks are crucial for long-term success in global markets.

Summary

Global selling has lots of benefits, like reaching more customers and boosting sales. It also makes your business more stable because you're not depending on just one market. Going global can spark new ideas and make your products better, and it can save money too. You might get access to special resources, like skilled workers or new technologies, and that can improve your products. Plus, selling worldwide helps protect your business from problems in one market.

But there are challenges too. Dealing with international rules and trade stuff can be tricky and expensive. Different cultures might lead to misunderstandings, so it's important to communicate well. Language differences can be a barrier too, so it's vital to overcome them. Managing how products move around the world and dealing with currency changes can be complicated. So, you need smart strategies to handle these challenges.

Chapter 2

Cultivating Adaptability and Flexibility: Navigating Cultural Differences and Market Nuances

Introduction

In the global marketplace, cultural differences and market intricacies play a significant role in shaping business interactions and success. To navigate these complexities effectively, it is essential to develop adaptability and flexibility. This chapter explores strategies for understanding and embracing cultural diversity, as well as adapting to market nuances, enabling you to thrive in international business environments.

2.1 Understanding Cultural Differences

Cultural differences matter in business. To succeed internationally, you need cultural intelligence. Here's what to keep in mind:

- **Cultural Awareness and Sensitivity:**

  Cultural awareness and sensitivity serve as the foundation for successful global interactions. This entails recognizing the vast variations in cultural norms, values, and beliefs that exist across countries and regions. An open mindset that respects diverse perspectives is paramount, as it not only helps prevent misunderstandings but also fosters positive relationships. Cultivating cultural sensitivity is the key to navigating the intricate tapestry of global culture, ensuring harmonious interactions.

- **Adapting Communication Styles:**

  Communication styles play a pivotal role in bridging cultural divides. Understanding the worldwide diversity in communication norms, including aspects like directness, non-verbal cues, and formality levels, is essential. Adapting your communication style to align with cultural expectations is crucial. Embracing practices such as active listening, asking clarifying questions, and seeking feedback serves as a bridge, promoting mutual understanding even in the face of diverse communication styles.

- **Mastering International Business Etiquette and Relationships:**

  The world of international business involves more than just transactions; it involves building meaningful relationships. Business etiquette and protocol are vital in this regard. Familiarizing yourself with local customs, from greetings to gift-giving practices, negotiation techniques, and meeting protocols, is essential. Demonstrating your knowledge of and respect for these local customs enhances your credibility and builds trust, laying the groundwork for fruitful international collaborations. Additionally, the art of building relationships should not be underestimated. In many cultures, investing time in personal connections and understanding the significance of networking and long-term business relationships is paramount.

Respecting local hierarchies and prioritizing face-to-face meetings whenever feasible further solidify these bonds, ensuring successful international partnerships.

2.2 Adapting to Market Nuances

The market is always changing, influenced by economics, politics, and society, which vary by region. Adapting your strategies to fit these differences is crucial for success. Remember these tips:

- **Market Research and Customization:**

  Cultural awareness and sensitivity serve as the foundation for successful global interactions. This entails recognizing the vast variations in cultural norms, values, and beliefs that exist across countries and regions. An open mindset that respects diverse perspectives is paramount, as it not only helps prevent misunderstandings but also fosters positive relationships. Cultivating cultural sensitivity is the key to navigating the intricate tapestry of global culture, ensuring harmonious interactions.

- **Pricing and Financial Considerations:**

  Communication styles play a pivotal role in bridging cultural divides. Understanding the worldwide diversity in communication norms, including aspects like directness, non-verbal cues, and formality levels, is essential. Adapting your communication style to align with cultural expectations is crucial. Embracing practices such as active listening, asking clarifying questions, and seeking feedback serves as a bridge, promoting mutual understanding even in the face of diverse communication styles.

- **Distribution, Logistics, and Legal Compliance:**

  To succeed in global business, it's crucial to navigate distribution channels and logistics effectively. This involves evaluating the best distribution channels for your target market, understanding local distribution networks, e-commerce platforms, and logistical challenges. It's also important to establish partnerships with reliable local distributors and explore efficient supply chain solutions.

Furthermore, legal and regulatory compliance is paramount. Take the time to familiarize yourself with local laws, regulations, and licensing requirements. Ensure compliance with product standards, protect intellectual property, and adhere to trade regulations. Seeking legal advice and engaging local experts can help you navigate complex legal landscapes, ensuring your global business operations run smoothly and within the bounds of the law.

2.3 Unlocking Success with Diversity, Inclusion, and Learning:

Embracing diversity and inclusion within your organization is like having a superpower for navigating cultural differences and market changes. Create a workplace where everyone feels valued and encouraged to work together. Use the unique strengths of a diverse team to adapt and come up with innovative ideas. Keep in mind that cultural differences and market trends aren't set in stone; they change over time. So, it's important to keep learning through research, connecting with others, and engaging with local communities. Adjust your strategies based on feedback, shifts in the market, and new trends to stay ahead. By promoting diversity, inclusion, and a commitment to always learning, your organization can thrive in the ever-changing global business world.

Summary

In the dynamic global business landscape, cultivating adaptability and flexibility is essential when navigating through cultural differences and market nuances. By understanding and embracing cultural diversity, adapting to market dynamics, and fostering an inclusive mindset, you can establish strong connections, build successful business relationships, and capitalize on international opportunities. Instead of thinking of problems as really hard roadblocks, it's better to see them as chances to get better and move forward. When we face challenges, it makes us come up with new ideas, change, and improve. It's like a spark that can ignite new and better ways of doing things, helping your business to grow.

Chapter 3

Overcoming Fear and Embracing Change: Stepping Out of Your Comfort Zone to Seize International Opportunities

Introduction

Setting out on a global selling adventure requires courage and a willingness to embrace change. Overcoming your fears and stepping out of your comfort zone are crucial steps in seizing international opportunities. This chapter offers strategies to conquer fear, welcome change, and unleash your potential to succeed in the global marketplace.

3.1 Overcoming Fear in Global Business (Fear of Failure, Unknown & Rejection)

Fear is a natural reaction when facing new and unfamiliar situations, often holding us back and limiting our growth. In international business, these fears can stop us from pursuing valuable opportunities. To overcome them:

- **Fear of Failure:**

  This fear often arises when we worry about making mistakes or not achieving our desired outcomes. In international business, it can manifest as a reluctance to take risks or try new strategies. However, seeing failure as a chance to learn and grow means understanding that setbacks are not permanent roadblocks but stepping stones to improvement.

- **Fear of the Unknown:**

  The unknown can be intimidating, especially in international markets where you may not fully understand the cultural nuances or market dynamics. However, embracing the unknown means recognizing that it holds vast potential for growth and new experiences.

- **Fear of Rejection:**

  This fear often stems from a fear of being judged or not meeting expectations. In international business, it can hinder your ability to engage with clients, partners, or customers from different cultural backgrounds. However, viewing rejection as an opportunity to improve and become more resilient reframes it as a constructive experience.

3.2 Embracing Change and Adaptability for Global Success

In the changing global market, adaptability is key. Adjusting strategies to match market shifts is crucial. Here's how:

- **Mindset Shift and Continuous Learning:**

  Cultivate a growth mindset that welcomes change as an opportunity for personal and professional development. Embrace change with a positive attitude, recognizing its potential for new possibilities and innovation. Invest in continuous personal and professional growth by actively seeking knowledge, staying updated on industry trends, and expanding your skill set through workshops, conferences, and online courses. The more you learn, the better equipped you'll be to navigate change.

- **Flexibility, Adaptability, and Stepping Out of Your Comfort Zone:**

  Develop the ability to pivot your strategies and adapt to new circumstances. Be receptive to feedback, consumer insights, and market trends. Foster a culture of flexibility within your organization, encouraging your team to embrace change and contribute innovative ideas. Challenge yourself to step outside of your comfort zone regularly by engaging in activities that push your boundaries. Whether it's attending networking events, participating in public speaking engagements, or embarking on international travel, gradually exposing yourself to new experiences builds resilience and expands your comfort zone, making you more adaptable in the face of change. Embracing these strategies wholeheartedly will enable you to navigate change effectively in the global business arena, positioning you for success.

3.3 Strategies for Managing Risk and Mitigating Fear

While embracing change is essential, effectively managing risks is equally crucial to mitigate fear. Begin with a proactive approach:

- **Risk Assessment and Planning:**

  Before venturing into new markets or making significant changes to your business, it's essential to conduct a thorough risk assessment. This means carefully looking at potential challenges that might come up during your expansion or transformation. This process acts like an early-warning system, helping you see the possible problems ahead of time and giving you a chance to get ready for them. By spotting these risks early, you not only protect your business from unexpected difficulties but also make sure your decision-making process is well-informed with lots of smart ideas.

- **Strategic Growth Through Collaborative Partnerships and Scaling:**

  Establishing strategic partnerships and alliances with local experts, distributors, or advisors experienced in the target market is a wise move. This approach provides valuable insights, support, and risk-sharing opportunities, effectively reducing the fear associated with entering new markets. Moreover, consider the complementary strategy of starting small and scaling. Initiate with a pilot project or test the waters in a specific region before full expansion. This method allows you to gather essential data, assess market responses, and make informed decisions while minimizing risk. As your confidence and experience grow, gradually scaling your operations becomes a more secure and less daunting path to sustainable growth.

Summary

Overcoming fear and embracing change are essential steps in seizing international opportunities as a global seller. By recognizing the impact of fear, embracing a growth mindset, and developing adaptability, you can navigate the global marketplace with confidence. Remember that stepping out of your comfort zone is where true growth and success lie. Embrace change as a catalyst for innovation, and fear as a stepping stone to resilience and achievement.

Chapter 4

Identifying Lucrative Markets: Conducting Comprehensive Market Research to Uncover Untapped Opportunities

Introduction

Market research lays the groundwork for successful global seller by guiding you to discover lucrative markets that offer untapped opportunities for growth. Conducting comprehensive market research is essential to gain insights into consumer needs, competition, and market dynamics. This chapter delves into strategies and methodologies for conducting effective market research, empowering you to pinpoint and capitalize on untapped market opportunities.

4.1 The Importance of Market Research

Market research is vital for global selling. It helps you understand markets, gauge demand, and make smart decisions. Here's why it's important:

- **Uncovering Market Potential and Understanding Consumer Behavior:**

  Market research uncovers hidden opportunities by revealing market gaps, unmet consumer needs, and emerging trends. This, in turn, enables you to identify high-growth target segments and tailor your products or services to their specific requirements. Moreover, effective market research doesn't stop at identifying potential; it delves deeper into understanding consumer behavior, preferences, and purchasing patterns. By shedding light on the factors that influence consumer decisions, market research empowers you to craft marketing strategies and offerings that seamlessly align with their expectations, enhancing your market penetration and customer satisfaction.

- **Assessing Competition and Mitigating Risks:**

  Thorough market research is like a treasure map for business success. It not only shows you who your competitors are but also reveals how they do business. With this knowledge, you can make your products or services stand out, create marketing that speaks to your customers, and avoid potential problems. It's like wearing armor against risks like crowded markets, economic changes, rules and regulations, and cultural differences. Understanding these risks helps you make smart choices and ensures a smoother path to success when entering new markets, allowing your business to grow and thrive.

4.2 Conducting Effective Market Research

To find good markets and new chances, you need to do thorough market research. Here's how to do it:

Define Clear Research Objectives

To start effective market research, first, be clear about what you want to find out. Decide what specific information you need, like how big the market is, who your customers are, what they like, or who your competitors are. This will help you stay on track and get useful results.

- **Primary Research:**

  This means getting information directly from the people you're interested in, like your potential customers. You can do this through surveys, talking to people, group discussions, or just observing them. Create questions or guides to help you gather the right information from customers, experts, and others involved.

- **Secondary Research:**

  In addition to talking to people, you can also find information that already exists from trustworthy sources like reports, studies, government info, or research done by others. Look for data on market trends, who lives where, how the economy is doing, and details about your competition. Useful sources for this can be found online, through industry groups, or in trade magazines.

Competitive Analysis, Market Segmentation, and Emerging Trends

Conduct a thorough analysis of your competitors, examining their market share, product offerings, pricing strategies, distribution channels, and marketing tactics. This analysis will help you identify gaps in the market that you can exploit. Further, segment the market based on relevant criteria such as demographics, psychographics, or geographic location. This segmentation allows you to target specific customer segments with tailored marketing strategies and offerings. Stay updated on emerging trends and technologies that could impact your target market by monitoring industry publications, attending conferences, and engaging with industry experts. This proactive approach helps you identify potential disruptors or innovative solutions that may create new market opportunities. Finally, in international markets, consider cultural factors and regulatory frameworks that significantly impact business operations. Adapt your strategies to align seamlessly with the cultural and regulatory context of the target market.

4.3 Analyzing and Applying Research Findings

Once you've gathered the necessary data, it's crucial to effectively analyze and apply the findings. Here's how:

- **Data Analysis:**

  Start by systematically organizing and analyzing the collected data using appropriate statistical methods, data visualization tools, or qualitative analysis techniques. Seek out discernible patterns, emerging trends, and key insights that can guide your decision-making process. For instance, data analysis may reveal that a particular customer segment is showing a growing preference for eco-friendly products, prompting you to consider incorporating sustainable practices into your offerings.

- **Strategic Decision-Making:**

  Based on the research findings, make well-informed decisions about market entry strategies, product development, pricing, distribution channels, and marketing campaigns. Develop a clear action plan that closely aligns with the identified opportunities while proactively addressing any potential challenges. For example, if research indicates a surge in e-commerce adoption within your target market, you might decide to prioritize online sales channels and tailor your marketing efforts accordingly.

Furthermore, maintaining a continuous watch over market fluctuations, shifts in consumer preferences, and competitor activities is paramount. Stay agile and be prepared to adapt your strategies as necessary, seizing emerging opportunities and responding effectively to shifts in the market landscape. Remember that market research is an ongoing process that empowers you to navigate the ever-evolving global business environment with precision and adaptability. By doing so, you position your business for sustainable growth and success in a dynamic global marketplace.

Summary

Identifying lucrative markets is a crucial step in global selling. Conducting comprehensive market research allows you to uncover untapped opportunities, understand consumer behaviour, assess competition, and mitigate potential risks. By following effective research methodologies, analysing findings, and applying the insights to your strategic decision-making, you can position yourself for success in the global marketplace. Stay vigilant, remain adaptable to market dynamics, and seize the untapped potential that awaits your business.

Serving Success at Dinner

Story 1

Hang on! I'm taking a quick pause to share an exciting story about my dear friend, Mr. Dinesh. Here's the story:

I have a very good friend named Mr. Dinesh, who has a successful clothing business in India. He has made quite a name for his business in the Indian market. However, he wanted to take their clothing brand to the global level. So, he decided to enter the Australian market to establish a new identity.

However, he only looked at the bright side of entering the Australian market and didn't pay much attention to the problems that might pop up. As a result, things didn't go as planned, and he ended up feeling really let down. The business suffered substantial losses, so much so that he even got into debt. All of this happened back in 2017.

One evening, he came over to my house for dinner, and as we chatted, he told me about his non-profit business, which made me feel really sorry for him. So, I decided to offer some advice. First, I talked to him about the not-so-great parts of doing business internationally. Then, I shared ideas on how to change those challenges into opportunities. We talked about important things like understanding different cultures, the little details that matter in various markets, how to communicate effectively, handling risks, embracing diversity, the importance of research, making products or services fit each market's needs, and managing money and pricing when doing business around the world.

He put these smart ideas into action in his business, and guess what? By the time the financial year came to an end, his business had grown by a whopping 20%! And the good news didn't stop there. Every year, that growth percentage kept getting bigger and better. Today, his business is doing incredibly well in the Australian market, and he's a real success story!

One day, my phone rang, and it was him on the line. He couldn't wait to share his big achievement with me. Hearing the great news filled me with joy and pride.

Chapter 5

Analyzing Competition: Studying the Global Landscape and Positioning Your Brand Effectively

Introduction

In the global marketplace, competition is fierce, making it essential for global sellers to analyze their competitors and position their brand effectively. By gaining insights into the global competitive landscape, identifying unique selling propositions, and developing a strong brand positioning strategy, you can differentiate yourself and capture the attention of your target audience. This chapter delves into effective strategies and techniques for analyzing competition and positioning your brand for success.

5.1 The Importance of Analyzing Competition

Watching your competition is crucial to understand the market, customer preferences, and industry trends, helping you make informed decisions and stand out effectively. Here's why competitive analysis is of paramount importance:

- **Identifying Competitive Advantages and Understanding Market Trends:** In-depth competitor analysis serves a dual purpose. Firstly, it helps identify your unique selling propositions (USPs) and competitive advantages, enabling you to emphasize what sets you apart and build a robust brand identity. Simultaneously, competitive analysis keeps you informed about market trends and industry evolutions. Monitoring competitors enables the identification of emerging trends, understanding customer demands, and detecting potential market gaps that can be skillfully exploited to your advantage.

- **Assessing Strengths, Weaknesses, and Benchmarking Performance:** In-depth competitor analysis empowers you to assess not only the strengths and weaknesses of your rivals but also their strategic moves and customer engagement tactics. Understanding their capabilities, product offerings, pricing strategies, and customer relationships allows you to strategically position your brand to capitalize effectively on their weaknesses and provide superior alternatives. Furthermore, benchmarking your performance against competitors isn't merely about setting goals; it's about gaining insights into industry-leading practices and best-in-class strategies. By measuring your performance against industry leaders, you can pinpoint areas for improvement, refine your strategies, and strive for excellence, ensuring your competitive edge in the market and continuously elevating your standards to meet or surpass industry benchmarks.

5.2 Analyzing Competitors

To effectively analyze your competition and position your brand, consider the following strategies:

- **Identifying Competitors and Conducting SWOT Analysis:** Commence your competitive analysis by identifying both direct and indirect competitors. Direct competitors offer similar products or services, targeting the same customer segments, and operating within the same geographic markets. In contrast, indirect competitors may present alternative solutions or cater to overlapping customer needs.

After identifying your competitors, delve into a comprehensive SWOT (Strengths, Weaknesses, Opportunities, Threats) analysis for each of them. This examination entails evaluating their strengths, which may include attributes such as product quality, market share, or effective distribution channels. Simultaneously, assess their weaknesses, such as having a limited customer base or outdated technology. It is also crucial to pinpoint opportunities they may be missing and to gauge the threats they pose to your business. By meticulously scrutinizing these aspects, you equip yourself with invaluable insights to inform your strategic decision-making and cultivate a competitive edge in the market.

- **Product, Pricing, Marketing, and Branding Analysis:**

  Expand your assessment to cover your competitors' product offerings, features, and pricing approaches. Investigate their products to discover opportunities for introducing innovative solutions to fill market gaps strategically. Evaluate whether your pricing is in line with market norms and explore the possibility of incorporating special value propositions to validate higher prices or differentiate through competitive pricing strategies.

Furthermore, delve into a thorough examination of your competitors' marketing and branding approaches. Analyze their messaging, brand positioning, target audience, and preferred communication channels. Identify their unique selling points and messaging tactics. This in-depth analysis not only enhances your understanding of market dynamics but also empowers you to refine your own marketing strategies and effectively position your brand for success in a competitive landscape.

- **Customer Experience, Industry Trends, and Innovation:** Complement your competitive analysis by conducting a comprehensive assessment of the customer experience delivered by your competitors. Scrutinize elements such as customer service, user experience, and post-purchase support. Through this evaluation, pinpoint areas where you can excel by providing exceptional customer experiences, ultimately setting your brand apart and nurturing customer loyalty.

Simultaneously, remain vigilant in monitoring industry trends, emerging technologies, and innovative practices within your sector. Identify the industry leaders pioneering innovation and closely examine their strategies. This proactive approach ensures that you stay at the forefront of industry developments, positioning your brand as an authoritative figure in your field and fostering a reputation for innovation and excellence.

5.3 Strategically Positioning Your Brand

After looking at what your competitors are doing and learning important stuff, the next big thing is to figure out how to make your brand special. Here are some ways to do it:

- **Brand Strategy Essentials: UVP, Segmentation, Differentiation:** To build a compelling brand strategy, start by defining your Unique Value Proposition (UVP), which highlights what sets your brand apart from competitors. Identify the unique aspects of your products or services and ensure clear communication of this value proposition to your target audience. Following that, perform Target Audience Segmentation based on demographics, psychographics, or other relevant criteria. Customize your messaging and marketing strategies for each segment, emphasizing how your brand meets their specific needs and desires. Lastly, create a Differentiation Blueprint that effectively communicates your brand's distinctiveness compared to the competition. Emphasize unique features, quality, customer service, or innovation to position your brand as the preferred choice for customers.
- **Brand Success Formula: Consistency and Continuous Innovation:** To strengthen your brand, maintain consistency across all touchpoints, including your website, social media platforms, packaging, and advertising. Create a unified brand identity that reflects your unique positioning and resonates with your target audience.

In addition to maintaining consistency, continuous innovation is key to staying competitive and relevant in a dynamic market landscape. Keep a vigilant eye on industry trends, actively seek and listen to customer feedback, and remain agile in adapting to emerging technologies. Regularly enhance your products, services, or customer experience to provide ongoing value and maintain your competitive edge. This commitment to innovation ensures that your brand not only survives but thrives in an ever-evolving business environment.

Summary

Analyzing competition and positioning your brand effectively are crucial steps in becoming a successful global seller. By understanding the competitive landscape, identifying your unique selling propositions, and developing a strong brand positioning strategy, you can differentiate your brand and attract customers in the global marketplace. Stay watchful, adapt to market dynamics, and continuously refine your strategies to stay ahead of the competition and establish your brand as a leader in your industry.

Chapter 6

Assessing Market Demand: Understanding Consumer Behavior and Adapting Your Products/Services Accordingly

Introduction

Assessing market demand is a critical aspect of becoming a successful global seller. Understanding consumer behavior, preferences, and needs allows you to tailor your products and services to meet their expectations. This chapter explores effective strategies for assessing market demand, conducting consumer research, and adapting your offerings to capture a larger share of the market.

6.1 The Significance of Assessing Market Demand

Figuring out what customers in the market want helps you tailor your products to their preferences, uncover fresh opportunities, and stay ahead of your competition. Here's why assessing market demand is crucial:

- **Customer Focus & Targeted Marketing:**

  Assessing market demand not only allows for the adoption of a customer-centric approach but also facilitates targeted marketing and positioning. Understanding customer preferences enables the development of tailored products and services, enhancing the overall customer experience and satisfaction. Simultaneously, by assessing market demand, you can pinpoint your target audience and their specific preferences, empowering you to create precise marketing campaigns and strategically position your offerings, ensuring that your messages align perfectly with the right audience. This dual benefit of market demand analysis amplifies your ability to connect with customers effectively and drive business success.

- **Market Demand-Driven Growth:**

  Product Improvement & Innovation: Through market demand assessment, you can pinpoint areas for improvement within your current product/service lineup by analyzing customer feedback and identifying pain points. This process enables you to refine and enhance your offerings, making them more competitive and appealing in the market. Additionally, market demand analysis serves as a valuable compass for new product or service development, helping you identify market gaps, emerging trends, and unmet consumer needs. Armed with this knowledge, you can innovate and introduce new offerings with a higher likelihood of success.

6.2 Conducting Consumer Research

To assess market demand effectively, consider implementing the following strategies for conducting consumer research:

- **Unlocking Consumer Insights:**

  Surveys, Groups, Interviews: In consumer research, we use different ways to learn from people. Surveys and questionnaires let us ask customers about what they like, how they shop, and what problems they face. This gives us lots of information, both numbers and personal stories, to help us make smart choices.

  Another way is by getting a bunch of regular people together to talk deeply about products or services. This is called a focus group. It helps us find detailed thoughts and honest feedback.

  And sometimes, we talk one-on-one with customers or experts to really dive deep into what drives them or what's new in the market. All of these methods help us understand what consumers want and how the market works.

Understanding Consumers: Analyzing Data, Listening on Social Media, and Testing Usability:

When we want to know more about the people we serve, we use three main ways.

- First, we look at data, like reports and what people say about us. This helps us find out what people like and how they act.
- Second, we pay attention to what people talk about on social media and in reviews. This helps us know what they think, what's new, and what our competitors are up to.

- And third, we watch how people use our stuff. This helps us see what's easy for them and what's not, so we can make things better.

All three of these ways help us understand our customers better, so we can give them what they want and do well in the market.

6.3 Adapting Your Products/Services

Once you have assessed market demand, it's essential to adapt your products or services accordingly. Here are the strategies to consider:

Tailoring, Enhancing, and Innovating Your Offerings for Market Demand: Adapting Your Business for Market Success: To thrive in the market, it's crucial to adjust what you offer. Start by customizing your products or services to fit what customers want. This means letting people personalize their purchases to match their needs. Listen to customer feedback and watch the market to keep improving your offerings. Make small, smart changes to fix problems, make things better, or add new features that match what customers want. Also, don't forget to be creative. Look for ways to make your products or services stand out with unique features, new tech, or cool designs that customers will love. By doing all this, your business will stay flexible, responsive, and in tune with what your customers want.

Optimizing Pricing Strategy and Effective Marketing Communication: In adapting to market demand, it's essential to consider your pricing strategy. Begin by assessing market conditions, taking into account factors such as perceived value, competitor pricing, and consumer willingness to pay. Aim to price your products or services competitively while ensuring profitability. Simultaneously, effective communication and marketing are crucial. Craft targeted marketing messages that highlight the benefits and value your offerings provide to consumers. Utilize consumer insights to create compelling marketing campaigns that resonate with your target audience and effectively communicate how your offerings meet their needs. This comprehensive approach ensures that your pricing aligns with market dynamics, while your communication strategy effectively connects with your audience, ultimately bolstering your competitiveness and market presence.

Summary

In the highly competitive global marketplace, the evaluation of market demand stands as a pivotal determinant of success. A profound understanding of consumer behaviors, preferences, and requirements equips you with the ability to skillfully adapt your products and services to effectively cater to market demands. By actively engaging in consumer research, data analysis, and ongoing enhancement of your offerings, you not only remain pertinent but also carve out a distinctive niche and secure a more substantial market share. It is imperative to remain receptive to consumer insights, foster innovation, and consistently uphold a customer-centric approach to secure enduring success on the global stage.

Strategy 3: Building a Strong Global Brand

Chapter 7

Crafting Your Brand Story: Developing a Compelling Narrative That Resonates with Global Audiences

Introduction

Crafting an impactful brand story is a powerful tool for global sellers to connect with their audiences and differentiate themselves in a crowded marketplace. A well-crafted brand story effectively communicates your values, purpose, and unique offerings, resonating with global audiences on an emotional level. In this chapter, we explore the strategies and techniques for developing a compelling brand narrative that engages and inspires your target customers.

7.1 The Power of a Brand Story

A brand story isn't just marketing jargon; it's a tale that captures your brand's soul, stirs feelings, and leaves a lasting mark. Here's why it's important:

Crafting a Compelling Brand Story:

For a successful brand, having an interesting brand story is super important, and it does two big things. First, it helps people feel a strong, emotional connection with your brand. It makes them relate to your story, feel empathy, and share similar values. This emotional connection is a big deal because it often guides people when they decide to buy things, leading them toward brands they feel close to.

Second, a well-made brand story does more than just stir emotions. It also shows why your brand is special and different from the others. It highlights your core values, mission, and the amazing stuff you offer to customers. This uniqueness not only helps you stand out in a crowded market but also carves a lasting place in the minds of people everywhere. Your brand becomes not just easy to remember but also really impactful.

When you put these things together, a compelling brand story becomes a super important tool for building a successful and memorable brand.

Creating a Strong Brand Story

Building Trust, Loyalty, and Staying Memorable: When it comes to your brand, having a great story does a lot of important things. First, it helps build trust and loyalty. When your brand story connects with what your customers believe in or care about, it makes them trust you more. And when you consistently do what your brand promises, you can keep those customers coming back and telling others how great you are.

But a good brand story does more than that. It also keeps your audience engaged and makes your brand hard to forget. It gets their attention, makes them curious, and leaves a lasting memory. When your brand is engaging like this, more people recognize it, tell their friends about it, and keep coming back for more. So, a compelling brand story is a super important tool for building trust, loyalty, and making sure people remember your brand.

7.2 Elements of a Compelling Brand Story

To create an engaging brand story for everyone worldwide, think about including these important parts:

The Power of a Compelling Brand Story

Authenticity, Origins, and Putting Customers First: Crafting a compelling brand story involves a few important steps. First, you need to figure out what your brand is all about and what it values. This helps make sure your story is true to your brand and what your audience cares about. Next, you can tell the story of how your brand started, including the founder's journey, what they care about, and why they started the brand. This personal touch makes your story more real and relatable. Finally, make sure your story is all about your customers. Show how your products or services help them with their problems or make their lives better. When you do this, it makes your customers the heroes of your story, and that's what connects with people the most. So, by putting these elements together, you can create a brand story that really speaks to your audience and makes them feel a strong connection.

Mastering the Art of Brand Storytelling: Emotion, Uniqueness, and Authenticity: Throughout the process of crafting an impactful brand story, several essential components come into play.

- **Emotion:**

  Your narrative should connect with your audience on a personal level by evoking emotions. Utilize storytelling techniques to create a compelling narrative that touches universal emotions such as joy, inspiration, nostalgia, or empathy. This emotional resonance will forge a deep connection with your global audience.

- **Uniqueness:**

  Highlight your Unique Selling Proposition (USP) within your brand story. Clearly articulate what distinguishes you from competitors and how your products or services offer unique value or solutions to specific problems. Build a strong case for why your brand is the best choice for your target audience.

- **Authenticity:**

  Authenticity and transparency are paramount. Building trust hinges on maintaining honesty and transparency in your brand story. Share not only your successes but also your challenges, demonstrating your commitment to continuous improvement. This genuine transparency fosters credibility and strengthens the bond with your audience.

7.3 Communicating Your Brand Story

Once you have crafted your brand story, it's crucial to effectively communicate it to your global audience. Consider the following strategies:

Effective Brand Communication

Consistency, Storytelling, and Multi-Channel Engagement: In the realm of brand communication, several key strategies are essential for effective storytelling and engagement. Firstly, consistency is vital in communicating your brand story. Ensure that your brand messaging aligns across all touchpoints, including your website, social media platforms, advertising, packaging, and customer interactions. Secondly, use storytelling techniques to engage your audience. Create a narrative arc, breathe life into compelling characters, and convey your brand message through captivating storytelling elements such as anecdotes, metaphors, or vivid visuals. Lastly, leverage a multi-channel approach to reach your global audience effectively. Harness the potential of social media, content marketing, influencer collaborations, public relations, and offline events to share your brand story and engage with your target customers.

Elevating Your Brand: The Power of Visual Storytelling and Audience Connection

When it comes to brand communication and engagement, employing a multifaceted approach is crucial. Firstly, elevate your brand story with visually captivating branding elements. Utilize colors, typography, imagery, and design that resonate with your brand's personality and message, ensuring visual consistency to enhance brand recognition and reinforce the core narrative. Secondly, actively engage and interact with your audience. Encourage their participation, promptly respond to their comments, feedback, and inquiries, and foster a genuine connection. Utilize social listening to gain insights into their reactions and incorporate their perspectives into your brand story, ensuring that it remains relevant and relatable.

Summary

The art of crafting a compelling brand story holds the potential to forge deep connections with global audiences and set your brand apart in the marketplace. By developing a narrative that captures your brand's identity, values, and unique offerings, you can establish an emotional connection, build trust, and inspire customer loyalty. Always remember, a well-crafted brand story goes beyond words – it engages emotions, sparks curiosity, and creates a lasting impact. Share your brand story consistently and authentically through various channels to effectively engage your global audience and leave a lasting impression.

Chapter 8

Localization and Cultural Sensitivity: Tailoring Your Brand Messaging and Visuals to Different Markets

Introduction

Expanding your business globally requires more than just a simple translation of your brand's messaging and visuals. To effectively engage and resonate with different markets, you must embrace localization and cultural sensitivity. This chapter delves into the strategies and considerations for tailoring your brand messaging and visuals to diverse markets, ensuring your global audience feels connected and understood.

8.1 The Importance of Localization and Cultural Sensitivity

Localization and cultural sensitivity are essential when entering new markets. Here's why they are crucial for global sellers:

- **Cultural Relevance:**

  Localization is like a special tool that helps your brand talk in a way that people in different places understand and like. It means changing your brand's words and pictures to match what the people there are used to and like. When you do this, it's like making a new friend because you can talk their way and understand the things they care about. This helps your brand become friends with more people around the world. It's kind of like learning to say "hello" in different languages or knowing what food someone likes. By doing this, your brand can connect with people on a deeper level, and that's super important when you want to be friends with people from all over the world.

- **Avoiding Misinterpretation**

  Imagine if your brand's words got all jumbled up and didn't make sense when they were translated into another language. That could cause big problems and make people not like your brand. But there's a way to avoid this! It's called localization, and it's like having a language expert make sure your brand's words and messages are clear and make sense to everyone. So, with localization, you can prevent confusion, keep things clear, and make sure your brand's message comes across just the way you want it to. It's like making sure your brand speaks the same language as your friends all around the world, so everyone can understand and like what you're saying.

8.2 Localization Strategies for Brand Messaging

When you're taking your brand to new places around the world, using localization strategies for your brand messaging is super important. Here are some things to think about:

- **Effective Language Adaptation and Cultural Context in Global Branding:**

  When expanding your brand globally, language adaptation is key. It's like having experts who understand both your language and the new one to ensure your brand messages are translated accurately and fit the new language and culture. This way, your brand sounds just right and avoids saying anything that might sound weird. Additionally, considering cultural context is vital. Before reaching out to people in a new place, take the time to learn about their customs, values, and what matters most to them. This ensures that when you communicate with them, it feels like you're not just speaking their language in words, but also in the things that truly matter to them, fostering a deeper connection.

- **Cultural Considerations in Brand Messaging and Storytelling for Global Expansion:**

  Firstly, think about your brand name and slogans. Check if they might have different meanings or unintended associations in the new places you're venturing into. Imagine if your brand name or slogans accidentally meant something strange or funny there. To avoid confusion or misunderstandings, it's crucial to adapt or even create entirely new brand names and slogans that fit well in each market.

Additionally, storytelling is a powerful tool for connecting with people in different cultures. When telling your brand's story, it's like weaving a tale that resonates with the way people in the new place tell stories. Use narratives, symbols, and metaphors that strike a chord with their cultural heritage. This way, your brand story becomes not just a story but a part of their culture, evoking emotions and forging a deep connection. It's like speaking to their hearts and making your brand meaningful to them.

8.3 Localization Strategies for Visuals

When taking your brand worldwide, focus on localizing your brand message. Here's what to think about:

- **Visual Branding Across Cultures:**

  Symbols, Colors, and Meanings: When you're expanding your brand globally, consider two vital factors. First, ensure that the pictures and symbols you use respect local beauty standards and cultural meanings. Use images that reflect the diversity and values of your audience while avoiding any visuals that could be misconstrued or offensive. Second, be mindful of colors and design elements, as different cultures perceive them differently. Conduct research to understand the cultural significance of your chosen colors and designs in your target regions. This way, your visuals will align with local preferences, preventing unintended misunderstandings and ensuring your brand resonates effectively.

- **Cultural Sensitivity in Visual Branding:**

  Representation and Graphics Localization: Firstly, when addressing models and representation, it's imperative to authentically reflect the rich ethnic, racial, and cultural diversity of your target audience. This entails steering clear of tokenism and stereotypes and instead embracing inclusivity in your visual content.

Additionally, as you delve into the localization of graphics and icons, it's crucial to undertake a meticulous evaluation of their cultural relevance within your communication. Adapt or replace these visual elements to harmonize with local preferences, ensuring they do not create confusion or appear out of sync with the target market's sensibilities. In essence, both aspects contribute to crafting a visual brand narrative that resonates genuinely and meaningfully.

8.4 User Experience Localization

When you're taking your brand to the global stage, focusing on user Experience localization becomes paramount. Here are some essential factors to consider:

- **Enhancing User Experience:**

  Interface, Navigation, and Time-Zone Sensitivity: In the world of User Experience Localization, simplicity is key. As you expand your brand globally, focus on creating a seamless and user-friendly experience. Customize your website, mobile apps, and digital platforms to match local preferences in design and navigation. This means making it easy for users to find what they need and interact with your content.

  Additionally, don't forget about time zones and dates – make sure your platforms display local times accurately to avoid any confusion or inconvenience for your global audience. This user-centered approach ensures that everyone, regardless of where they are, can effortlessly connect with your brand.

  Remember, a great user experience transcends language and borders, making your brand more accessible and appealing to a diverse audience worldwide.

- **Payment Methods and Currency:**

  Enhancing the user experience extends beyond language and design; it's also about making transactions effortless for your global audience. Consider offering localized payment methods and currencies that align with the preferences of diverse markets. To achieve this, take the initiative to familiarize yourself with local payment preferences, and seamlessly integrate the most appropriate payment gateways into your platform. This proactive approach not only simplifies transactions but also demonstrates your commitment to meeting the unique needs of customers worldwide. By providing a convenient and user-friendly payment experience, you can strengthen trust and satisfaction among your global user base, contributing to the success of your brand on a global scale.

8.5 Testing and Iteration

In the realm of testing and iteration, a continuous improvement approach is essential:

- **User Feedback**

  Collecting feedback from your audience is a pivotal step in ensuring the success of your localization efforts. Engage in user testing with representatives from your target market to comprehensively evaluate the effectiveness of your localized brand messaging and visuals. Listen attentively to their insights and recommendations, recognizing their unique perspectives on cultural nuances and preferences. Incorporate this invaluable feedback to continually refine and enhance your content, ultimately achieving a higher level of cultural sensitivity and resonance with your global audience. This iterative approach not only fosters an inclusive and authentic brand presence but also strengthens your connection with diverse markets.

- **Continuous Iteration:**

  In the dynamic landscape of localization, it's essential to recognize that the process is ongoing. Regularly monitor the performance of your localized content, paying close attention to user engagement metrics and feedback. Embrace adaptability by being ready to adjust your strategies based on these insights. Moreover, maintain a vigilant stance toward evolving cultural trends and changes, ensuring that your brand remains not only relevant but also responsive to the ever-changing global landscape. This commitment to continuous iteration enables your brand to stay in sync with diverse markets and their evolving needs, ultimately fostering lasting resonance and success.

Summary

Localization and cultural sensitivity are critical for global sellers aiming to connect with diverse markets. By tailoring your brand messaging and visuals to the cultural preferences, values, and aspirations of your target audience, you can create a deeper connection, foster trust, and avoid misinterpretations. Embrace localization as a strategic approach, investing in professional translation services, cultural research, and user testing to ensure your brand resonates authentically with global audiences. By demonstrating cultural sensitivity, you can cultivate strong relationships, drive engagement, and ultimately succeed in the global marketplace.

Mentoring in Milan

Story 2: Wait! Wait! Wait! I know you guys are very engaged in reading, but I thought that sharing another interesting story would make it more engaging and attractive to read.

Last year, I had the opportunity to attend a business event in Milan, Italy, where I had the pleasure of meeting Mr. Paul, a well-known local businessman who had achieved significant success in the toy industry. Mr. Paul shared his ambitious plans to expand his business internationally, and what excited me the most was his intention to kickstart this expansion by entering the Indian market. He firmly believed that India, with its status as a developing nation and its immense population, offered the ideal starting point for his global venture.

What's truly amazing is that Mr. Paul had been getting ready for this big move for the last two years. He spent a lot of time studying the Indian market and making detailed plans. But there was one big problem that was standing in his way—the Chinese market was really strong in the toy business. Plus, there was heavy competition in the Indian market and lots of other companies in India making innovative toys, which was making it tough for him to get started there.

He asked me for help with this challenge, and I felt really proud to be able to help. I came up with a plan to tackle all these problems, and he decided to use it in his business strategy when entering the Indian market. At first, he wasn't too sure about my plan, but when he saw the results, he was not only surprised but also super happy with how things turned out.

He sent me an email to share this fantastic news and how excited he was. He also said he wanted to meet me in person when he came to India. I was thrilled to receive his message and happily agreed. The next month, we met as planned, had long discussions, and celebrated his success together.

Chapter 9

Leveraging Digital Platforms: Harnessing the Power of Social Media, E-commerce, and Online Marketing

Introduction

In today's digital age, global sellers have unprecedented opportunities to reach a vast audience through various online platforms. This chapter explores the strategies and techniques for leveraging digital platforms effectively. From social media to e-commerce and online marketing, we delve into the power of these tools and how they can propel your business to new heights in the global marketplace.

9.1 The Advantages of Digital Platforms

Digital platforms offer numerous advantages for global sellers. Here's why harnessing their power is crucial:

- **Wide Reach & Targeted Marketing:**

  Digital platforms offer wide-reaching opportunities by enabling you to connect with a global audience without geographical limitations, harnessing the internet's ubiquity for exponential market expansion. Additionally, they empower targeted marketing through advanced precision, enabling you to tailor your efforts to specific demographics, interests, and behaviors, ultimately enhancing engagement and conversion rates. This strategic approach not only boosts ROI but also allows you to track and analyze data in real-time, refining your marketing strategies for even greater success in the dynamic digital landscape.

- **Cost-Efficiency and Data-Driven Excellence in Marketing:**

  Digital platforms not only provide wide-reaching opportunities and precision targeting but also offer cost-effective options, making them accessible to businesses of all sizes when compared to traditional marketing channels. With careful planning and optimization, significant results can be achieved within a limited budget. Additionally, these platforms grant access to valuable data and analytics, offering insights into user behavior, preferences, and campaign performance. This data-driven approach empowers businesses to fine-tune their strategies, optimize campaigns, and make well-informed decisions, further enhancing their overall marketing effectiveness and ROI.

9.2 Mastering Social Media for Global Selling

Learn smart ways to use social media to reach people all over the world. Here are some important things to think about:

- **Platform Selection & Content Strategy:**

  In the realm of social media, platform selection is pivotal for global sellers. It involves identifying social media platforms that align with your target audience's preferences and demographics, including popular choices like Facebook, Instagram, LinkedIn, Twitter, and YouTube. However, comprehensive research is essential to understand which platforms your audience actively engages with. Concurrently, crafting an effective content strategy is vital for connecting with your global audience. This strategy should encompass a diverse array of engaging and informative content, spanning visuals, videos, blog posts, user-generated content, and interactive elements. Customizing your content to suit each platform's format and meet its audience's expectations is the key to international success.

- **Influencer Marketing & Community Engagement:** Collaborate with influencers who align with your target market to broaden your brand's reach and credibility, harnessing their authentic connection with their audience to amplify your message. Choose influencers that share your brand values and genuinely connect with their followers. Additionally, actively engage with your social media community by promptly responding to comments, messages, and reviews, showing that you value their feedback and input. Encourage user-generated content, organize exciting contests, and facilitate meaningful conversations to not only build a dedicated and active community around your brand but also to foster a sense of belonging and loyalty among your followers. These strategies, when executed effectively, can transform your social media presence into a powerful tool for global brand growth.

9.3 E-commerce Strategies

Expanding globally with e-commerce: Discover effective ways to use e-commerce strategically and connect with a worldwide audience. Here are some important points to keep in mind:

- **User-Friendly Website & Mobile Optimization:**

  To supercharge your e-commerce efforts, make a user-friendly website your top priority. Ensure it loads swiftly, boasts intuitive navigation, and adapts seamlessly to various devices. Streamline the buying process, provide secure payment options, and consider catering to your audience with localized language and currency choices. Furthermore, don't overlook the significance of mobile optimization, given the increasing prevalence of mobile shopping. Consider creating a mobile-responsive website or even investing in a dedicated mobile app to enhance user experiences and significantly boost your conversion rates. Embracing these strategies is pivotal for thriving in today's competitive e-commerce landscape.

- **Enhancing E-commerce:**

  Personalization, Recommendations, and Seamless Fulfillment: To ensure success in e-commerce, start by tailoring the user experience based on individual preferences and behaviors, implementing personalization strategies. Utilize recommendation engines to suggest relevant products or services, increasing the potential for upselling and cross-selling. Additionally, streamline the order fulfillment process to guarantee timely delivery and exceptional customer service. Offer multiple shipping options, enable order tracking capabilities, and engage in proactive communication with customers to build trust and foster loyalty.

9.4 Online Marketing Techniques

Expanding global reach with online marketing is crucial in today's global marketplace. Explore key strategies for reaching a global audience effectively:

- **Search Engine Optimization (SEO) & Pay-Per-Click Advertising (PPC):**

  To effectively expand your online presence, start by optimizing your website and content for search engines to enhance organic visibility. Conduct thorough keyword research, consistently produce high-quality content, optimize meta tags, and actively build backlinks to boost your website's search engine rankings. Furthermore, leverage the potential of pay-per-click advertising (PPC) platforms like Google Ads and social media advertising to precisely target specific keywords, demographics, and geographical locations. Create persuasive ad copies, establish clear campaign objectives, and implement a regular cycle of analysis and optimization to maximize your return on investment (ROI). By combining these strategies, you can navigate the dynamic digital landscape successfully and reach a broader audience with your online marketing efforts.

- **Content & Email Marketing:**

  In the realm of online marketing, begin by creating valuable and informative content that addresses your audience's pain points and establishes your brand as an industry expert. This can include publishing blog posts, whitepapers, case studies, and videos to provide insights and solutions, thereby driving brand awareness and credibility. Additionally, consider the power of email marketing. Build an email list of interested prospects and existing customers and develop targeted email campaigns that nurture leads, promote new products or offers, and encourage repeat purchases. Personalize your email communications to enhance engagement and boost conversions, ensuring a comprehensive online marketing strategy that effectively connects with your audience.

Summary

Digital platforms have revolutionized the way global sellers connect with their audience, promote their products/services, and drive growth. By effectively harnessing the power of social media, e-commerce, and online marketing, you can expand your reach, engage with your target audience, and maximize your business's potential. Embrace the opportunities provided by these platforms, stay abreast of the latest trends and best practices, and continuously optimize your strategies to thrive in the dynamic digital landscape. In simple terms, digital platforms are incredibly powerful. They've changed how businesses connect with customers, promote their stuff, and thrive globally. By making the most of these online opportunities, you can take your business to new levels, reach customers worldwide, and achieve impressive growth and success.

Strategy 4: International Logistics and Supply Chain Management

Chapter 10

Understanding Logistics: Streamlining the Process of Shipping, Customs, and Delivery

Introduction

Efficient logistics operations are essential for global sellers to ensure smooth shipping, customs clearance, and timely delivery of products to customers worldwide. This chapter dives into the complexities of logistics and provides insights on streamlining the process. By understanding the key components and optimizing logistics operations, you can enhance customer satisfaction, reduce expenses, and gain a competitive edge in the global marketplace.

10.1 The Importance of Efficient Logistics

Efficient logistics operations bring forth several benefits for global sellers:

- **Customer Satisfaction & Cost Optimization:**

  In the domain of logistics, customer satisfaction is paramount. Ensuring timely delivery, accurate tracking, and smooth customs clearance all play pivotal roles in fostering a positive customer experience. Efficient logistics operations guarantee that customers receive their orders promptly, ultimately leading to heightened satisfaction and fostering repeat business. Additionally, cost optimization is a crucial aspect of logistics management. By streamlining operations, you can minimize shipping costs, reduce delays, and prevent unnecessary expenses stemming from errors, inefficiencies, or supply chain disruptions. This optimization not only enhances profitability but also enables you to offer competitive pricing, strengthening your overall logistics strategy.

- **Competitive Advantage & Global Expansion Facilitation:**

  Efficient logistics operations not only differentiate your brand from competitors but also facilitate global expansion by ensuring reliable and efficient shipping and delivery experiences, establishing a reputation for dependability, and enabling successful entry into new international markets. Understanding shipping intricacies, customs procedures, and local regulations is key to overcoming logistical barriers and expanding your reach effectively. Moreover, these streamlined logistics can lead to cost savings, allowing you to invest in further improving customer experiences and staying ahead in the competitive landscape.

10.2 Key Components of Logistics

Key Considerations for the Components of Logistics you should follow:

- **Shipping & Custom Clearance:**

  In the realm of logistics management, it's essential to navigate the key components effectively. This includes understanding various shipping methods such as air freight, sea freight, and land transportation, and evaluating their pros and cons concerning cost, speed, and the nature of products. Establishing relationships with reliable shipping carriers or freight forwarders is crucial for ensuring efficient transportation. Furthermore, when it comes to customs clearance, familiarity with customs regulations and documentation in target markets is essential. This involves proper preparation of shipping documents, including commercial invoices, packing lists, and certificates of origin, and partnering with customs brokers or agents to efficiently navigate the complexities of customs clearance.

- **Last-Mile Delivery, Warehousing and Inventory Management:**

  In the context of logistics, optimizing warehousing and inventory management is crucial. This involves minimizing costs and ensuring timely order fulfillment through the implementation of inventory tracking systems, stock rotation prioritization, and efficient storage layouts. The consideration of utilizing fulfillment centers or third-party logistics providers can further streamline operations. Additionally, efficient last-mile delivery is essential for customer satisfaction. To achieve this, establish partnerships with reliable local couriers or postal services in different markets to ensure efficient and timely deliveries. Enhance transparency and customer expectations management by leveraging tracking technologies and providing real-time shipment updates throughout the delivery process."

10.3 Streamlining Logistics Operations

It means making things work better and cost less by making the logistics process simpler and smarter. Key considerations include:

- **Supply Chain Visibility, Collaboration and Strategic Alliances:**

  In the domain of streamlining logistics operations, two critical components come to the forefront. First, supply chain visibility takes center stage. It involves investments in cutting-edge technologies and systems that provide real-time visibility into your supply chain. This entails the utilization of track-and-trace solutions, IoT devices, and data analytics to monitor inventory levels, track shipments, and swiftly identify any bottlenecks or inefficiencies.

  Secondly, collaboration and strategic alliances play a pivotal role. Establishing strong partnerships with shipping carriers, freight forwarders, customs brokers, and logistics service providers is crucial. Through close collaboration, objectives are aligned, processes streamlined, and their expertise leveraged to optimize logistics operations effectively. These two components, supply chain visibility and strategic collaboration, form the backbone of streamlined logistics.

- **Data-Driven Decision Making, Automation and Technology Integration:**

  In the quest to boost logistics efficiency, two key factors stand out. First, data-driven decision-making takes the spotlight. This means using data analysis to make smart decisions and continuously improve logistics. By closely examining things like delivery time, order accuracy, and transportation costs, companies can spot areas to make things better and put data-driven plans into action.

Secondly, automation and tech integration play a crucial role. Automating logistics processes is a must. Using systems like inventory management, warehouse management, and order management that work smoothly with your e-commerce platform is vital. Automation not only cuts down on mistakes but also boosts efficiency, making your logistics work well. This modern approach ensures accuracy, efficiency, and cost-effectiveness in your logistics, ready to meet global demands.

Summary

Efficient logistics operations are critical for global sellers to meet customer expectations, reduce costs, and gain a competitive edge. By understanding the key components of logistics and streamlining processes related to shipping, customs clearance, and delivery, you can optimize your supply chain and enhance customer satisfaction. Embrace technology, forge strategic partnerships, and leverage data analytics to continuously improve your logistics operations and position your business for success in the global marketplace.

Chapter 11

Selecting International Partners: Finding Reliable Distributors, Suppliers, and Logistics Providers

Introduction

Expanding into the global marketplace often requires collaborating with international partners such as distributors, suppliers, and logistics providers. The art of choosing the right partners is crucial for global sellers to ensure smooth operations, establish a strong presence in foreign markets, and deliver value to customers. In this chapter, we embark on a journey to dissect the process of cherry-picking international partners, offering insights on finding reliable and trustworthy collaborators.

11.1 The Importance of Selecting Reliable Partners

Selecting reliable partners is vital for global sellers due to the following reasons:

- **Market Expertise & Expansion:**

  Partnering with local experts during global expansion brings significant benefits. They offer vital knowledge about the target market, helping you navigate regulations, tailor strategies, adapt products, and understand customer needs. Collaborating with established partners accelerates market entry, boosts brand visibility, and leverages existing networks for a strong presence. Together, these efforts streamline expansion, enhance growth, and open doors for joint marketing, co-branding, and resource sharing, strengthening your position in diverse global markets.

- **Operational Efficiency & Risk Mitigation:**

  In the global market expansion journey, having reliable partners plays a crucial role in ensuring smooth operations and reducing risks. These trusted collaborators significantly contribute to operational efficiency by consistently providing reliable and timely services, be it in product distribution, raw material supply, or logistics and warehousing management. Partnering with such efficient allies streamlines supply chain operations, fosters operational excellence, and ultimately boosts overall customer satisfaction. Moreover, relying on dependable partners significantly lowers the chances of disruptions, such as supply chain delays, quality fluctuations, or subpar customer support. Their unwavering dependability acts as a robust safety net against potential risks, providing a strong foundation for sustained long-term growth and success in the global arena.

11.2 Identifying Potential Partners

When looking for potential partners, it's crucial to do thorough research and due diligence:

- **Partner Selection:**

  Research, Due Diligence, and Reputation: Conduct a rigorous investigation to pinpoint potential partners who closely align with your business objectives, target markets, and industry prerequisites. This involves leveraging industry directories, engaging with trade associations, exploring online platforms, and seeking referrals to amass a comprehensive dossier about prospective partners.

Simultaneously, delve into the reputation and track record of potential partners. Scrutinize their historical performance, peruse client testimonials, delve into case studies, and evaluate online reviews. Keep a keen eye out for indicators of reliability, professionalism, and the proven ability to deliver on commitments. This dual approach ensures that you not only identify partners who align with your strategic goals but also those who have a proven track record of excellence and trustworthiness.

- **Strategic Partner Selection:**

  Compatibility, Alignment, and Financial Stability: When choosing strategic partners, consider some crucial factors. Start by checking if potential partners share your company's values, culture, and goals. Make sure their mission, vision, and how they do business match yours, forming a solid foundation for a mutually beneficial partnership. Also, look into their financial stability to see if they can support your business effectively. This involves analyzing their financial statements, checking credit reports, and having honest discussions about their financial health and commitment to long-lasting partnerships. These evaluations help you pick partners who not only fit your strategic plans but also have the stability and shared values needed for a successful collaboration.

11.3 Selecting Reliable Distributors

When it comes to the selection of dependable distributors, several key considerations should be taken into account:

- **Market Coverage:**

  When evaluating potential distributors, it's crucial to delve into their distribution network and market reach. Examine their capabilities in accessing and penetrating your target markets effectively. This assessment should encompass an evaluation of their distribution channels, geographical reach, and the strategies they employ to connect with your audience. Additionally, consider their presence in various retail outlets, e-commerce platforms, and their proficiency in implementing effective marketing strategies to maximize market coverage and brand visibility.

- **Sales Expertise & After-Sales Support:**

  When evaluating potential distributors, it's crucial to consider two fundamental aspects. Firstly, assess their sales expertise and capabilities, looking for partners who possess a deep understanding of your product or industry, maintain strong retailer relationships, and boast a proven track record of driving sales and expanding market share. Secondly, scrutinize the quality of after-sales support provided by these distributors. Rigorously evaluate their ability to handle customer inquiries, offer technical assistance, and proficiently manage product warranties. Recognize that effective after-sales support significantly contributes to bolstering customer satisfaction and fostering enduring brand loyalty.

11.4 Selecting Reliable Suppliers

When selecting reliable suppliers, there are important factors to think about:

- **Quality Assurance & Supply Capacity:**

  Firstly, emphasize the importance of quality assurance. Ensure that potential suppliers have robust quality assurance processes, adhere to industry standards, hold certifications, and are dedicated to delivering consistent product quality. To substantiate their quality claims, request product samples and conduct comprehensive testing.

  Simultaneously, consider the supply capacity of these suppliers to meet your business demands. Evaluate their production capabilities, inventory management systems, and their ability to scale production as your business expands. While doing so, be cautious about over-reliance on a single supplier and inquire about their contingency plans to address potential disruptions. Balancing these considerations is essential for securing reliable suppliers in your global expansion endeavors.

- **Ethical and Sustainable Practices:**

  Examine the ethical and sustainable practices of potential suppliers with a discerning eye. Scrutinize their dedication to environmental sustainability, fair labor practices, and adherence to social responsibility standards. Partnering with suppliers who not only meet your quality and quantity requirements but also share your values can create a compelling narrative for your brand. It showcases your commitment to responsible and ethical business practices, resonating positively with environmentally and socially conscious consumers while reinforcing your brand's reputation as a conscientious global player.

11.5 Selecting Reliable Logistics Providers

When considering the choice of reliable logistics providers, it's crucial to focus on the following key aspects:

- **Coverage and Network:**

  When selecting logistics partners, a thorough assessment of their coverage and network is essential. Investigate the geographical extent of their operations, the variety of transportation modes they employ, and their track record in handling international shipments. Collaborating with partners who possess expansive networks and specialized expertise tailored to your target markets not only ensures dependable service but also bolsters your global presence, facilitating efficient operations, and driving market expansion. This strategic partnership not only optimizes logistics but also paves the way for a more extensive market reach, ultimately contributing to the growth and success of your global endeavors.

Track Record and Performance: First, think about where they can deliver, how they deliver things, and if they have experience with sending things to other countries. It's a good idea to work with partners who know a lot about the places you want to reach and can deliver things there efficiently. Assess the track record and performance of potential logistics providers.

Second, check how well these logistics partners have done in the past. See if they usually deliver things on time, handle customs paperwork well, keep you informed about where your shipments are, and make their customers happy. You can also ask them for references from other people they've worked with. These things help you choose partners who not only fit your plans but also are trustworthy and share your values for a successful partnership.

- **Technology and Systems:**

  Evaluate the technology and systems used by potential logistics providers. Look for partners who employ advanced tracking systems, provide real-time visibility into shipments, offer efficient communication channels, prioritize data security, and have a robust contingency plan for addressing technological disruptions. If their systems can seamlessly integrate with yours, it can make operations run more smoothly, improve collaboration, and enhance the security and resilience of your supply chain.

Summary

Selecting reliable international partners is a critical step for global sellers seeking success in foreign markets. By conducting thorough research, assessing reputations, aligning values, and evaluating capabilities, you can identify trustworthy distributors, suppliers, and logistics providers. Collaborating with reliable partners enhances operational efficiency, facilitates market expansion, and mitigates risks. Go for partners who are on the same page with your business goals and share your commitment to delivering value to customers.

Chapter 12

Optimizing Inventory Management: Balancing Supply and Demand Across Different Markets

Introduction

Effective inventory management is crucial for global sellers to meet customer demand, minimize costs, and maintain a competitive edge. Balancing supply and demand across different markets requires careful planning, forecasting, and efficient inventory control strategies. In this chapter, we delve into the intricacies of optimizing inventory management and provide insights on how to achieve a harmonious balance between supply and demand in the global marketplace.

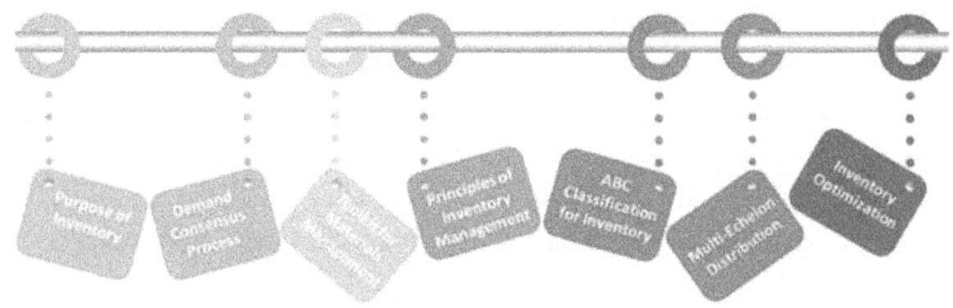

12.1 The Importance of Optimizing Inventory Management

Optimizing inventory management offers several benefits for global sellers:

- **Customer Satisfaction & Cost Efficiency:**

  Effective inventory management plays a pivotal role in achieving two critical business objectives. Firstly, it fosters customer satisfaction by guaranteeing the availability of the right products at the right time, thus minimizing stockouts, boosting order fulfillment rates, and facilitating timely deliveries, all of which collectively elevate the overall customer experience. Additionally, it helps build customer loyalty, as customers are more likely to return to a business that consistently meets their product needs. Secondly, it enhances cost efficiency by striking a harmonious equilibrium between inventory levels and customer demand, thereby reducing holding costs, mitigating the risks associated with obsolete inventory, and ultimately lowering operational expenses, culminating in cost optimization and improved profitability. This, in turn, frees up capital that can be reinvested in growth initiatives or used to further enhance customer service, creating a virtuous cycle of customer satisfaction and financial success.

- **Demand Planning and Forecasting Accuracy:**

  Effective inventory management relies on accurate demand planning and forecasting. By carefully analyzing market trends, customer preferences, and past sales data, businesses can predict shifts in demand and adjust their inventory levels accordingly. This helps prevent situations where you have too much or too little stock on hand. When you get this right, it not only keeps customers happy by ensuring products are available when they want them but also saves money by avoiding excess inventory or missed sales opportunities. So, good inventory management, based on solid demand forecasting, is not just about customer satisfaction but also about smart resource use and better decision-making in the supply chain, giving businesses a competitive edge.

- **Supply Chain Efficiency:**

  Good inventory management means keeping the right amount of stuff in stock by looking at what customers want and what you've sold before. This helps make customers happy because they get what they need when they want it, and it saves money by not having too much or too little stuff. It also makes it easier to get products from suppliers to customers quickly and smoothly, which is important in today's fast business world. So, it's not just about making customers happy; it's also about using resources wisely and making the whole process work better.

12.2 Strategies for Optimizing Inventory Management

Global sellers can benefit in various ways by using strategies to improve inventory management. Here are a few of them:

- **Demand Forecasting, Safety Stock and Reorder Points:**

  For efficient inventory management and a smooth supply chain, start with robust demand forecasting. Use historical sales data, market research, customer feedback, and industry trends to estimate future demand accurately. Employ forecasting tools for precision. Set safety stock levels to guard against demand shifts and supply chain disruptions. Calculate optimal reorder points, considering lead times, demand fluctuations, and service goals. Regularly review and adjust these levels to stay agile and responsive to market changes, ensuring efficient inventory management.

- **Just-In-Time (JIT) Inventory Management:**

  Embrace the effectiveness of Just-In-Time (JIT) inventory management to reduce inventory holding costs and enhance operational efficiency. By aligning production and delivery schedules closely with suppliers, you can efficiently meet customer demand without accumulating excess inventory, thus optimizing resource allocation. Real-time inventory tracking systems add an extra layer of control by providing visibility into stock levels and facilitating timely restocking, ensuring that your inventory remains finely tuned to meet the dynamic demands of your business environment.

- **ABC Analysis and SKU Rationalization**

  Enhance your inventory management with two crucial strategies. Begin with ABC analysis, which categorizes products based on their value and sales volume. Prioritize high-value items for meticulous management and employ specific strategies for low-value or slow-moving products to use resources efficiently and boost returns. Next, consider SKU rationalization to streamline your product lineup. By reducing product variations and simplifying inventory complexities, SKU rationalization improves operational efficiency and enhances inventory management. When you combine these strategies, you create an organized and cost-effective approach to optimize your inventory.

- **Collaboration with Suppliers:**

  In the pursuit of efficient inventory management, it's imperative to foster strong collaboration with your suppliers. Establish effective communication channels that enable the sharing of demand forecasts and the synchronization of production schedules. By cultivating mutually beneficial partnerships grounded in principles of agility, flexibility, and timely restocking, you not only prevent the pitfalls of stockouts but also avoid accumulating excessive inventory. This collaborative approach strengthens the entire supply chain, ensuring that your inventory management remains responsive and aligned with market dynamics, ultimately enhancing customer satisfaction and cost-effectiveness.

12.3 Technology and Tools for Inventory Optimization

Here are some key considerations to follow when it comes to enhancing inventory efficiency through technology and tools:

- **Inventory Management Systems:**

  In the realm of optimizing inventory management, consider the adoption of state-of-the-art inventory management systems. These systems offer real-time visibility into inventory levels, enhancing your ability to track and manage your stock efficiently. They also streamline order processing, reducing errors and delays, while automating replenishment workflows to ensure timely restocking. Harness the power of data analytics within these systems to fine-tune your inventory levels, identify market trends, and make informed, data-driven decisions. With such systems in place, you can significantly improve the precision and efficiency of your inventory management processes, ultimately contributing to better customer satisfaction and cost optimization.

- **Collaboration Platforms:**

  In your pursuit of effective inventory management, consider the integration of advanced collaboration platforms into your operations. These platforms serve as powerful tools to bolster communication and coordination not only within your organization but also with suppliers, distributors, and logistics partners. By providing real-time information sharing capabilities, they enhance visibility across the supply chain, fostering greater accuracy in demand forecasting and promoting seamless collaboration.

- **RFID and Barcode Technology:**

  Enhance your inventory management by employing RFID (Radio Frequency Identification) and barcode technology. These advanced tools are pivotal for accurate and efficient inventory tracking. They enable real-time visibility into your inventory, ensuring you have an up-to-the-minute understanding of stock levels. Moreover, they effectively reduce manual errors, saving time and resources while significantly enhancing overall inventory accuracy. With RFID and barcode technology, you can revolutionize your inventory management processes, making them more precise and streamlined.

- **Data Analytics and AI:**

  In addition to advanced tracking technologies, leverage the power of data analytics and AI-driven tools to further elevate your inventory management. These cutting-edge tools empower you to extract valuable insights from diverse data sources, including sales data, customer behavior, and market trends. By harnessing the potential of data analytics and AI, you can achieve more accurate demand forecasting, optimizing inventory levels to match actual demand, and streamline decision-making processes. Ultimately, this integration of data analytics and AI enhances the efficiency and effectiveness of your inventory management, leading to cost savings and improved customer satisfaction.

Summary

To conclude, the optimization of inventory management is a necessity for global sellers looking to thrive in the competitive global marketplace. By implementing effective demand forecasting, judicious safety stock usage, Just-In-Time principles, SKU rationalization, and harnessing technology, you can achieve a harmonious supply-demand balance. This strategic approach significantly impacts your entire business, resulting in efficient operations, heightened customer satisfaction, cost efficiency, and improved supply chain performance. These collective benefits are paramount for ensuring the continued success and growth of your global selling operations, guaranteeing your relevance and profitability in the ever-evolving global landscape.

A Takeoff to Success

Story 3

Here I am again! I hope you guys are enjoying reading this book. And now, I would like to introduce you to the story of one of my juniors.

Once upon a time, I was going for a holiday trip in South India. During the flight, I happened to sit beside a friendly traveler named Mr. Rakesh Juneja. As we chatted, we realized we had something special in common – we were both graduates of the same college, with him being a junior to me. Our conversation revolved around our college experiences and a bit about our businesses. Mr. Juneja informed me that he was en route to Karnataka to receive an award. He kindly extended an invitation for me to join him, despite my vacation plans. I couldn't resist his offer, so a couple of days later, we met again.

During an event, Mr. Juneja was called on stage to deliver a speech. It was then that I learned about his successful business in utensil manufacturing in India and his ambitious dream of expanding internationally. His insights piqued my curiosity, and during the closing ceremony that evening, I couldn't hold back my questions any longer.

Mr. Juneja explained his strategies and plans for taking his business to a global level. I was impressed by his thoroughness, especially considering the pitfalls many businesses face when entering global markets due to lack of expertise. He mentioned his shortcomings in logistics, customs, and distribution, as well as a need for assistance in understanding legal regulations.

Given my experience in helping other businesses thrive in global markets, I extended a helping hand to Mr. Juneja. After all, we shared the same alma mater. I assisted him from the basics of customs procedures and compliance with regulations to connecting him with reliable distributors. To my surprise, he made remarkable progress within just six months of entering the international market. He not only survived but thrived, successfully establishing an Indian brand presence in a market previously dominated by other companies.

Witnessing his global success up close filled me with immense pride.

Chapter 13

Creating a Global Sales Strategy: Establishing Effective Distribution Channels and Sales Networks

Introduction

Creating a comprehensive global sales strategy is crucial for reaching customers in different markets, expanding your business, and maximizing revenue potential. Establishing effective distribution channels and sales networks plays a vital role in successfully penetrating international markets. In this chapter, we explore the key elements of creating a global sales strategy and provide insights on building robust distribution channels and sales networks.

13.1 The Importance of a Global Sales Strategy

A well-defined global sales strategy offers several advantages:

- **Market Penetration and Revenue Generation in Global Sales Strategy:**

  When expanding your market reach, a robust global sales strategy is essential. Market penetration involves identifying target customer segments, understanding their unique needs, and tailoring your approach to meet those requirements. This positions your products or services effectively and sets you apart from competitors. Simultaneously, effective revenue generation is optimized through this strategy by capitalizing on sales opportunities across multiple markets. Utilizing various distribution channels and sales networks allows you to tap into a broader customer base and drive sales growth, strengthening your global business.

- **Scalability, Efficiency, and Customer Relations in Global Sales Strategy:**

  A robust global sales strategy has two vital aspects. First, it ensures scalability and efficiency by standardizing procedures, using technology, and leveraging sales networks, facilitating success across diverse markets. Second, it prioritizes customer relationship management, focusing on understanding customer needs, offering tailored solutions, and delivering exceptional service consistently. This customer-centric approach fosters loyalty and enduring partnerships, forming the foundation for success in the global business arena.

13.2 Building Distribution Channels

Discover the key elements of building effective distribution channels:

- **Market Research and Analysis:**

  Conduct in-depth market research to identify the most suitable distribution channels for your target markets. This process involves conducting thorough research to identify the most suitable distribution channels for your target markets. Dive into market characteristics to understand the market's dynamics, examine customer preferences to tailor your offerings effectively, navigate the competitive landscape to find your unique positioning, and scrutinize regulatory requirements to ensure compliance.

- **Global Sales Expansion Strategies:**

  Direct vs. Indirect Approaches: When expanding globally, you have two fundamental approaches to consider. Firstly, contemplate implementing a direct sales strategy, which enables you to retain full control over the customer experience and how your brand is represented. This can involve establishing your in-house sales team or utilizing e-commerce platforms to directly engage with customers across different markets. Secondly, explore indirect sales methods by forming partnerships with distributors, agents, wholesalers, or retailers. These partnerships allow you to leverage their existing networks and established market presence. When assessing potential partners, evaluate their market reach, industry expertise, customer base, and alignment with your brand values and objectives to ensure a mutually beneficial collaboration in your global sales expansion.

- **Online Marketplaces:**

  Harness the power of online marketplaces like Amazon, eBay, Alibaba, or local e-commerce platforms to not only expand your market reach but also access a diverse and global customer base. These platforms offer more than just convenience; they come with built-in infrastructure that simplifies market entry, instill trust among customers due to their established reputation, and present valuable marketing opportunities to promote your products or services effectively. This strategic utilization of online marketplaces can significantly bolster your business's ability to thrive and grow in new and established markets alike.

13.3 Developing Sales Networks

Consider these essential steps to build a successful sales network:

- **Strategies for Effective Channel Partner Selection and Training & Support:**

  When it comes to building a successful sales network, consider two fundamental aspects. First, carefully select your channel partners based on their expertise, market reach, reputation, and alignment with your business goals. Establish clear expectations, mutual objectives, and robust support mechanisms to foster successful collaborations. Second, prioritize comprehensive training and ongoing support for your channel partners, ensuring they possess a deep understanding of your products or services, effective sales techniques, and high customer service standards. Consistent communication and knowledge sharing are key elements in constructing a strong sales network.

- **Incentives, Rewards and Relationship Management:**

  In the realm of optimizing your sales network, you can focus on two more key aspects. One, introduce incentive programs and reward structures to effectively motivate and incentivize your sales network. This could encompass various strategies such as offering sales commissions, bonuses, performance-based rewards, or recognition programs. Recognizing and rewarding high-performing partners not only nurtures loyalty but also acts as a catalyst for ongoing growth. Two, prioritize relationship management within your sales network. This entails maintaining regular communication, providing timely information and resources, and actively seeking feedback. These efforts are integral to strengthening collaboration, addressing challenges, and uncovering opportunities for improvement within your sales network, ultimately contributing to its overall prosperity.

13.4 Technology and Tools for Sales Enablement

Leveraging technology and sales enablement tools can significantly boost the effectiveness of your sales strategy. These resources are instrumental components:

- **Customer Relationship Management (CRM) Systems:**

  Elevate your business operations by implementing a robust Customer Relationship Management (CRM) system. This cutting-edge technology empowers you to efficiently manage and organize customer data, monitor and analyze sales activities, and track all customer interactions seamlessly.

  Incorporating a CRM system not only streamlines your sales processes but also facilitates better communication within your team and with your customers. By harnessing the power of data-driven insights, you can proactively address customer needs, personalize interactions, and build stronger, more lasting relationships with your clientele. Experience a new level of efficiency and effectiveness in your customer relationship management endeavors with a CRM system at your disposal.

- **Sales Analytics & Sales Enablement Tools:**

  Harness the power of sales analytics tools to extract invaluable insights into your sales performance, market dynamics, and customer behavior, enabling you to spot sales opportunities, refine strategies, and make data-driven decisions that fuel sales growth. Additionally, leverage sales enablement tools like sales content management platforms, proposal generators, and sales training platforms to empower your sales force. These resources offer convenient access to pertinent sales materials, streamline proposal creation, and facilitate ongoing learning and skill enhancement, ultimately equipping your team for greater success.

Summary

In conclusion, creating a comprehensive global sales strategy is crucial for expanding your business and tapping into international market revenue potential. By establishing efficient distribution channels, nurturing sales networks, and leveraging technology and resources, you can firmly establish your brand globally, ensuring sustained sales growth. A well-executed global sales strategy not only enhances customer engagement and value delivery but also builds lasting relationships, driving the success of your global sales initiatives.

Chapter 14

Localization of Marketing Campaigns: Adapting Advertising and Promotional Activities to Resonate with Local Customers

Introduction

Localization of marketing campaigns is vital for global sellers to effectively connect with customers in different markets. Adapting advertising and promotional activities to resonate with local customers ensures that your messaging is culturally relevant, relatable, and impactful. In this chapter, we delve into the nuances of localizing marketing campaigns and provide insights on how to successfully engage and connect with diverse audiences around the world.

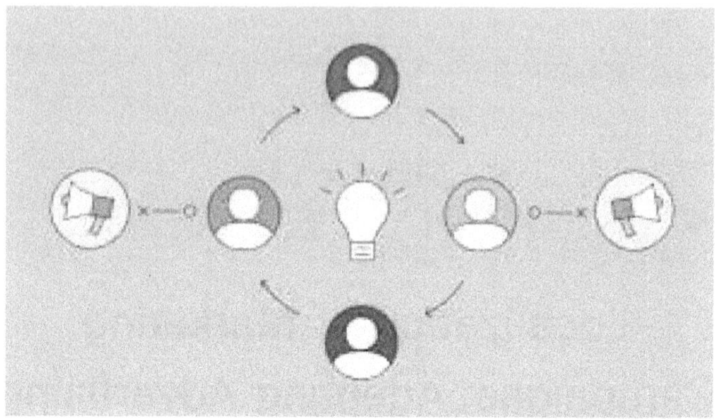

14.1 The Importance of Localization in Marketing Campaigns

Localization offers several benefits for global sellers:

- **Cultural Relevance & Language Adaptation**

  Cultural relevance is vital for marketing success. Localization aligns your messages with local norms, values, and preferences, building trust and meaningful connections. Language adaptation, especially accurate translations and suitable styles, boosts communication. It conveys familiarity and cultural respect, enhancing engagement in local markets. Timing matters too; tailoring campaigns to cultural events or trends resonates with your audience. Staying attuned to cultural shifts and local feedback ensures ongoing marketing refinement, keeping it relevant and effective.

- **Targeted Communication & Brand Perception:**

  Achieving success in marketing requires targeted communication. Localization empowers you to tailor your messaging to cater to the precise needs, desires, and aspirations of the local customer base. By comprehending local market dynamics and consumer behavior, you can craft campaigns that resonate deeply and drive heightened customer engagement. Beyond this, a localized marketing campaign goes a long way in showcasing your commitment to understanding and serving local customers, positioning your brand as not only relevant but also trustworthy and customer-centric. This, in turn, significantly enhances brand perception, bolstering the likelihood of customer loyalty and advocacy.

14.2 Strategies for Localizing Marketing Campaigns

Explore the following strategies to tailor marketing campaigns to a local audience:

- **Market Research:**

  Begin by conducting thorough market research to gain insights into the local culture, consumer behavior, market trends, and competitive landscape. Identify the unique characteristics and preferences of the target market to inform your campaign localization efforts. By embracing these insights, you can not only refine your messaging but also adapt product offerings or services to better suit local needs, ensuring your marketing strategy is not only culturally sensitive but also aligned with the evolving demands of the market. This proactive approach to localization, grounded in comprehensive research, establishes a strong foundation for sustainable success in local markets, fostering lasting customer relationships and driving business growth.

- **Message Adaptation and Visual Elements:**

  When adapting your marketing for different cultures, focus on two key areas: your message and visuals. To tailor your message effectively, consider language, humor, and social norms in the local culture. Make sure your content resonates with the values and preferences of the target audience. Additionally, pay attention to visual elements like colors and symbols, as different cultures may interpret them differently. Ensure that your visuals not only align with the local culture but also appeal to the local audience's aesthetic sensibilities. This thoughtful approach to localization helps you connect with customers from diverse backgrounds, avoid misinterpretations, and ultimately enhance the effectiveness of your marketing efforts.

- **Connecting Locally:**

  Influencers, Celebrities, and Social Media: To boost your marketing, think about collaborating with local influencers or celebrities who hold sway in the target market. Their endorsement can add credibility to your brand, boost visibility, and create a stronger bond with local customers. Furthermore, when it comes to social media, make sure to adapt your strategies for the local audience. Get to know the popular social media platforms in the target market and tailor your content formats, engagement methods, and posting schedules to match local preferences. By doing so, you'll be able to forge deeper connections with your audience at the local level, ultimately enhancing the effectiveness of your marketing efforts.

14.3 Digital Advertising Localization

Explore the following strategies for localizing digital advertising:

- **Search Engine Optimization (SEO) & Pay-Per-Click (PPC) Advertising:**

  Incorporate effective strategies for digital advertising localization. First, implement tailored SEO techniques that align with the target market's language and search patterns, optimizing website content, metadata, and keyword selection to enhance visibility on local search engines and increase organic traffic. Additionally, for Pay-Per-Click (PPC) advertising, customize campaigns for local audiences by targeting pertinent keywords and refining ad copies to resonate with local language, preferences, and cultural nuances. This approach guarantees that your ads are presented to the most relevant audience, precisely when it matters most.

- **Social Media Advertising:**

  Craft a robust digital advertising strategy by utilizing social media advertising to effectively reach your ideal audience within your target market. Customize your ads to resonate with local trends and preferences, ensuring they not only capture attention but also drive higher engagement and conversions. By harnessing the potential of social media, you can connect with a specific audience and make your advertising efforts more personalized and impactful within your chosen localization efforts. Additionally, regularly analyzing your advertising performance and adjusting your approach based on feedback and data insights will help you refine your strategy for even greater success.

14.4 Measuring and Evaluating Campaign Performance

- **Take a closer look at these options for assessing and evaluating campaign effectiveness:**

  Data Analytics: Forge a robust digital advertising strategy by harnessing the potential of social media advertising to precisely reach your target audience within your desired market. Customize your ads to resonate with local trends and preferences, ensuring they not only capture attention but also drive higher engagement and conversions. By utilizing data analytics tools, you can effectively measure the performance of your localized marketing campaigns. Keep a close eye on key metrics such as engagement rates, conversion rates, and return on investment (ROI) to assess campaign effectiveness and make data-driven adjustments for continual improvement. This proactive approach ensures that your advertising strategy remains dynamic and finely tuned for optimum results.

- **Customer Feedback & Continuous Optimization:** For successful localized marketing, ask local customers what they think. Use surveys, check social media, and welcome their reviews to understand what they like and make improvements they'll appreciate. Keep refining your campaigns using data and feedback. Try out different things and change your ads as needed to stay relevant and effective. This way, your marketing stays flexible and in sync with what's happening locally.

Additionally, consider keeping an eye on important numbers to see how your changes are working. Look at things like how many people are engaging with your ads, how many are buying, and whether your spending is making you more money. This helps you make smart decisions and fine-tune your marketing to keep it effective and in line with what your local audience wants.

Summary

Localization of marketing campaigns is crucial for global sellers to effectively engage and connect with local customers. By understanding the cultural context, adapting messages and visuals, leveraging local influencers, and optimizing digital advertising strategies, you can create impactful and resonant campaigns. Continuously measure and evaluate campaign performance, gather customer feedback, and make data-driven adjustments to ensure ongoing success. By prioritizing localization, you can build brand loyalty, drive customer engagement, and achieve marketing excellence in diverse markets around the world.

Chapter 15

Influencer Marketing and Partnerships: Leveraging Influential Personalities and Brands to Expand Your Reach

Introduction

Influencer marketing has emerged as a powerful strategy for global sellers to expand their reach and connect with target audiences. By partnering with influential personalities and brands, you can leverage their credibility, authority, and reach to promote your products or services. Within the pages of this chapter, we will delve into the intricacies of influencer marketing and partnerships, providing valuable insights on how to effectively collaborate with influencers and brands to maximize your marketing efforts.

15.1 The Power of Influencer Marketing

Achieve influencer marketing success with these tried-and-true strategies:

- **Trust and Authenticity:**

  Influencers have cultivated devoted followings through trustworthiness and authenticity. By forming partnerships with the right influencers, you can harness their credibility and foster trust within their audience. This trust not only boosts brand recognition and customer loyalty but also translates into a tangible increase in purchase intent. Building genuine connections through influencers can amplify your brand's impact and establish a lasting rapport with your target audience, ultimately driving sustained business growth.

- **Targeted Reach:**

  Influencers have a knack for understanding their followers and can be your secret weapon in reaching the right audience. They're experts at connecting with specific groups and niches, so teaming up with them means your message lands directly where it matters most. It's akin to having a personal channel to your ideal customers, which not only boosts the effectiveness of your marketing but also fosters deeper connections with your audience. This can lead to increased engagement, trust, and long-lasting customer relationships, paving the way for your brand to flourish in a genuinely impactful manner.

- **Content Creation and Storytelling:**

  Influencers are masters at crafting compelling content and weaving captivating stories. With their unique perspectives and creative flair, they possess the ability to authentically showcase your products or services, generating a genuine connection with their audience that can drive not only interest but also higher conversion rates. Partnering with influencers in content creation and storytelling opens up the opportunity for your brand to be portrayed in an engaging and relatable manner, establishing a memorable presence in the hearts and minds of potential customers. This, in turn, paves the way for lasting brand loyalty and advocacy.

- **Amplification and Virality:**

  Influencers can be your brand's best promoters. Their devoted followers often share their content, giving your brand a chance to be seen by more people on social media and other online places. This sharing can lead to a snowball effect, where your brand's message spreads quickly, gaining more visibility and making it a hot topic online. It's like having a team of brand advocates working to get the word out and create a buzz around your products or services.

15.2 Selecting the Right Influencers

When choosing the ideal influencer for a successful marketing campaign using these established strategies, consider these essential factors:

- **Relevance and Alignment:**

  When choosing influencers, it's crucial to find those whose audience and content align with your brand values, target market, and marketing objectives. Look for influencers who have a real passion for your industry and can genuinely embody your brand's essence, creating an authentic connection with your audience. This alignment ensures that your influencer partnerships yield the best results for your marketing efforts.

- **Reach and Engagement:**

  When assessing potential influencers, it's important to check how many followers they have and the level of interaction their posts receive, such as likes, comments, and shares. Yet, don't overlook the significance of meaningful engagement, like authentic conversations and interactions, as it indicates a genuinely interested and active audience. This comprehensive evaluation ensures that the influencers you select are not only popular but also capable of fostering valuable connections with your brand, making a meaningful contribution to your marketing success.

- **Building Authentic and Enduring Influencer Partnerships:**

  When you're looking at potential influencers, it's essential to check if they're genuine and trustworthy. You can do this by examining the kind of content they create, paying attention to what their audience says, and seeing how they've worked with other brands in the past. Look for influencers who always keep things open, honest, and real when they connect with their followers. Also, think about the idea of forming long-lasting partnerships with influencers who could become strong supporters and advocates for your brand. These ongoing relationships allow for more in-depth collaboration, creating content together, and making influencer marketing a natural part of your strategy. This not only boosts the impact of your campaigns but also fosters genuine and lasting connections with your audience, reinforcing your brand's position in the market.

15.3 Collaboration and Campaign Execution

When planning a collaborative marketing campaign and executing it using these proven strategies, keep these key factors in mind:

- **Clear Objectives and Guidelines:**

  For a successful campaign, it's essential to have clear goals and provide influencers with straightforward rules to follow. Offer influencers a detailed guide that explains your campaign objectives, the messages you want to convey, and any specific content requirements. This ensures everyone understands the mission and maintains consistency. Additionally, keep the lines of communication open with influencers, welcoming questions and addressing concerns promptly to facilitate a smooth and collaborative campaign execution. This way, you can work together seamlessly to achieve your marketing goals.

- **Co-Creation of Content:**

  When working with influencers, join forces to craft content that reflects their personal style and speaks to their audience. This partnership is all about authenticity and letting influencers express their creativity while staying true to your brand's values. It's like a creative collaboration that adds a unique touch to your campaigns, making them more engaging and relatable to your target audience. By co-creating content, you tap into the influencer's expertise, ensuring your message resonates effectively with their followers.

- **FTC Compliance & Performance Measurement:**

  When working with influencers, make sure they follow advertising rules like those from the FTC to maintain trust. Ask influencers to clearly show when they're promoting something. Also, set up ways to measure how well your influencer campaigns are doing. Check things like how many people see your content, how they engage with it, how many visit your website, and how many actually buy your products. This helps you know if your influencer marketing is both legal and effective. Plus, it allows you to make improvements based on what works best for your brand and your audience, ensuring your marketing stays on the right track for continued growth and success. By staying compliant and data-driven, you can adapt your influencer strategies to stay ahead in the ever-evolving marketing landscape.

Summary

To sum it up, influencer marketing is a powerful strategy for global sellers looking to expand their reach and connect with target audiences. Partnering with influencers taps into their credibility, authenticity, and broad reach to promote your products or services effectively. By selecting the right influencers, setting clear goals, collaborating on content, ensuring compliance with FTC rules, and tracking performance indicators, you can harness influencer marketing's potential to amplify your brand message, build trust, generate buzz, and achieve tangible outcomes. It's a dynamic approach that resonates with audiences, propelling your marketing efforts to new heights in the ever-evolving global commerce landscape.

Strategy 6: Effective Communication and Negotiation

Chapter 16

Cross-Cultural Communication: Mastering Language Barriers and Non-Verbal Cues

Introduction

In a globalized world, effective cross-cultural communication is essential for global sellers to navigate diverse markets and build meaningful connections with customers. This chapter explores the intricacies of cross-cultural communication, focusing on overcoming language barriers and understanding non-verbal cues. By mastering these aspects, you can enhance communication effectiveness, foster trust, and establish successful business relationships across cultures.

16.1 Language Barriers in Cross-Cultural Communication

Let's explore the vital role of language in facilitating cross-cultural communication within our globalized world:

- **The Importance of Language:**

  Language is not merely a means of conveying thoughts and feelings; it is the cornerstone of effective human interaction. It serves as the very essence of our shared existence, enabling us to bridge gaps, forge connections, and create a sense of belonging. In the context of cross-cultural communication, its importance becomes even more pronounced, as it becomes the compass guiding us through the intricate web of diversity in our globalized society.

  In a world where people of different backgrounds, languages, and traditions constantly intersect, language serves as both a unifying force and a source of richness.

It allows us to embrace the uniqueness of each culture while finding common ground in the human experience. The ability to communicate across cultural boundaries not only facilitates cooperation but also deepens our understanding of the world and enriches our personal growth.

- **Translations and Localization:**

  In the ever-expanding global marketplace, precise and culturally sensitive communication is paramount. This entails ensuring accurate translations of your marketing materials, product descriptions, and customer support documentation. To accomplish this, it is imperative to partner with professional translators who are not only fluent in the target language but also possess a profound understanding of the local culture. By doing so, you not only convey your message appropriately but also foster a deeper connection with your diverse audience, transcending linguistic barriers to create meaningful engagement.

- **Cultural Sensitivity & Language Support:**

  In our interconnected world, it's crucial to understand the little things that can make a big difference in communication—like cultural cues and language nuances. Being aware of gestures, idioms, and tone helps avoid misunderstandings. When you go the extra mile to provide language support, such as multilingual customer service and translated product info, it not only shows you're inclusive but also makes connecting with a diverse customer base easier. This strengthens your global presence, fosters stronger customer relationships, and ultimately enhances your brand's reputation as one that truly understands and values its global audience.

16.2 Non-Verbal Communication in Cross-Cultural Communication

Non-Verbal Communication in Cross-Cultural Contexts holds significant importance in our interconnected global society. Let's explore its pivotal role and understand how it contributes to our success in the globalized world:

- **Importance of Non-Verbal Cues:**

  Non-verbal cues play a significant role in communication, often conveying emotions, attitudes, and intentions. Proficiency in understanding and interpreting non-verbal cues is essential for effective cross-cultural communication, as cultural variations can influence their meaning. Mastery of non-verbal communication not only bridges cultural gaps but also facilitates empathy and mutual understanding, promoting harmonious interactions across diverse backgrounds and enhancing our ability to thrive in today's global society.

- **Body Language and Gestures:**

  To excel in cross-cultural communication, it's vital to familiarize yourself with the body language and gestures commonly used in the target culture. This awareness goes beyond simply recognizing the physical actions; it involves understanding the deeper cultural connotations attached to these gestures. These nuances can vary widely across different regions and may hold distinct interpretations or significance within each culture.

Being mindful of these cultural connotations is crucial, as it not only helps avoid misunderstandings but also showcases your respect for and understanding of the subtleties that define effective global communication.

- **Eye Contact, Personal Space and Touch:**

  Understanding the nuances of non-verbal communication is crucial in cross-cultural interactions. Eye contact, for instance, varies across cultures, with some viewing it as a sign of respect and engagement, while others perceive it as confrontational. Adapt your approach to eye contact based on cultural expectations. Similarly, be mindful of personal space and touch boundaries, which can vary widely. While some cultures embrace close physical proximity and frequent touching, others prefer more personal space. Respect these cultural norms to ensure respectful and comfortable interactions across diverse backgrounds.

16.3 Effective Cross-Cultural Communication Strategies

Uncover the vital role of cross-cultural communication in our globalized society:

- **Cultural Awareness and Sensitivity:**

  To understand different cultures better, start by learning about their customs, values, and social norms. Put yourself in their shoes to feel what they feel and adjust how you communicate to respect their differences. This not only helps prevent misunderstandings but also promotes harmony and open-mindedness in our diverse, interconnected world. It's a step towards building stronger connections and fostering a sense of unity in our global community.

- **Active Listening, Clarification and Confirmation:**

  Listening actively by paying attention to both words and body language, asking questions, and displaying genuine interest is key. To enhance clarity and prevent misunderstandings, summarize and paraphrase information. This ensures that both parties share a common understanding of the conversation's content and objectives, fostering stronger connections in cross-cultural communication. These practices not only bridge cultural gaps but also promote empathy and meaningful exchanges across diverse backgrounds.

- **Patience and Flexibility:**

  In navigating cultural differences, it's important to exercise patience and adaptability in your communication approach. Keep an open mind, listen actively to understand, and strive to discover common ground that can bridge gaps and foster strong, meaningful relationships. Embracing these practices not only enhances communication but also promotes empathy and connection across diverse backgrounds, making for a richer global experience.

Summary

Mastering cross-cultural communication is essential for global sellers to effectively engage with customers from diverse backgrounds. By overcoming language barriers, ensuring accurate translations, and understanding non-verbal cues, you can enhance communication effectiveness and build trust. Embrace cultural sensitivity, practice active listening, and remain flexible to navigate cross-cultural communication challenges successfully. With these strategies, you can foster meaningful connections, establish strong business relationships, and thrive in the global marketplace. - Negotiating international deals: Navigating negotiation tactics and cultural norms.

Chapter 17

Building Trust and Long-Term Relationships: Fostering Strong Partnerships with International Clients and Stakeholders

Introduction

uilding trust and cultivating long-term relationships is vital for global sellers to succeed in the international marketplace. In this chapter, we explore the importance of trust, unveil effective strategies for building and maintaining trust, and how to foster strong partnerships with international clients and stakeholders. By prioritizing trust and nurturing relationships, you can establish a solid foundation for business growth and sustainable success.

17.1 The Importance of Trust in International Business

The crucial role of trust in the business world:

- **Trust as a Foundation:**

  Trust is not just a foundational element; it's the bedrock upon which successful business relationships are built. It serves as the bedrock that inspires confidence in your partners and colleagues, fostering a spirit of collaboration that's essential for success. Trust is the lubricant that makes effective communication flow smoothly, and without it, establishing long-term partnerships and achieving mutual success can feel like an uphill battle. Therefore, nurturing trust is not merely an option but a vital strategy for thriving in the world of business.

- **Building Credibility and Reputation:**

  Building trust in the business world hinges on two critical pillars: credibility and reputation. These factors are instrumental in establishing lasting and meaningful connections. It begins with the consistent delivery of promises, where reliability becomes your calling card. Transparency further strengthens your position, as it showcases openness and honesty in your dealings. Beyond this, embracing ethical business practices solidifies your standing, demonstrating your commitment to integrity and responsible conduct. Through these actions, you not only build credibility but also craft a favorable reputation that resonates in the global marketplace. These qualities are not just assets; they are the bedrock upon which thriving business relationships and long-term success are built.

- **Trust and Risk Mitigation:**

  Trust emerges as a powerful force in international business, not only as a bridge between parties but as a potent tool for risk mitigation. When clients and stakeholders place their trust in your brand, it goes beyond mere confidence; it becomes the foundation of enduring commitments. This trust encourages the sharing of sensitive information, the willingness to navigate challenges together, and a commitment to the long term. In doing so, it effectively reduces the overall risk associated with international business transactions. Consequently, trust isn't just a relational asset; it's a strategic tool that fosters sustainable partnerships and lays the groundwork for long-term success in the global marketplace.

- **Trust as a Competitive Advantage:**

  Earning trust isn't just a valuable asset; it's a strategic game-changer in the global market. When clients and stakeholders have confidence in your brand, they are more inclined to choose you as their partner. Trust signifies not only reliability and integrity but also a steadfast commitment to delivering exceptional value. By establishing trust, you set yourself apart from competitors, creating a loyal and dedicated client base that can be your strongest advocate in the competitive global landscape.

17.2 Strategies for Building Trust

Elevate your business to the next level by implementing the following strategies:

- **Consistency and Reliability:**

  Consistently delivering on promises and maintaining a high level of reliability is essential for building trust. To build and maintain trust, consistency is key. Ensure that your promises are consistently delivered upon, and maintain a high level of reliability in all aspects of your business. Whether it's your products, services, or customer support, strive to consistently meet or exceed expectations. This unwavering commitment fosters confidence in your brand, reinforcing your reputation as a trustworthy partner in the global market.

- **Transparency and Open Communication:**

  Trust is like a sturdy foundation, and it's constructed through two simple but powerful tools: being open and talking openly. In business, this means sharing how things work, what things cost, and the rules you follow. It also means encouraging transparency in conversations with your clients and partners, listening to their worries, and keeping them in the loop with timely updates. This not only builds trust but also strengthens your relationships, making your business a reliable and trustworthy choice in the eyes of your stakeholders.

- **Relationship Building:**

  Invest time and effort in relationship building activities. Attend industry events, actively participate in networking opportunities, and engage in thoughtful conversations to establish personal connections with clients and stakeholders. These connections not only form the basis of trust but also serve as the driving force behind the development of enduring, mutually beneficial partnerships that can propel your business forward.

- **Cultural Understanding and Respect:**

  In the world of international business, trust thrives when you understand and respect different cultures. Take the time to learn about the norms and communication styles of your clients and partners. Adjust your approach to show genuine respect for their cultural preferences. This cultural sensitivity not only builds trust but also lays the groundwork for strong and enduring international relationships, opening doors to opportunities you may not have otherwise discovered.

17.3 Nurturing Long-Term Relationships

Ensure the longevity of your relationship by incorporating these essential guidelines:

- **Proactive Relationship Management:**

  Cultivate strong and lasting connections with clients and stakeholders through proactive engagement. Initiate regular communication to not only gather feedback and address concerns promptly but also to collaboratively identify opportunities for growth and improvement. By consistently demonstrating your commitment to their success, you not only solidify existing partnerships but also create an environment where innovation and mutually beneficial initiatives can thrive, ultimately propelling both parties towards greater achievements.

- **Customized Solutions and Personalization:**

  Tailoring your solutions and services to meet the specific needs of your clients and stakeholders is like fitting a glove to a hand – it shows that you not only understand their unique challenges and objectives but also genuinely care about their success. This level of customization not only strengthens your connection with them but also forges a bond of trust and reliability. By collaborating closely and continuously adapting to their evolving requirements, you create a partnership that's not just resilient and supportive but also primed for innovation and long-term prosperity.

- **Value Creation and Collaboration:**

  Focus on creating substantial value for your clients and stakeholders. Actively seek opportunities for collaboration, sharing knowledge, and embarking on joint initiatives. By working hand-in-hand to achieve common objectives, you solidify a sense of partnership and strengthen the foundation of trust upon which your relationships are built. This cooperative spirit not only enhances the present but also sets the stage for a future filled with shared success and continued growth.

- **Conflict Resolution and Problem-Solving:**

  Effectively address conflicts and challenges with a proactive problem-solving approach, aiming for win-win solutions. Transparency and fairness not only resolve immediate issues but also bolster trust, emphasizing your commitment to long-term, mutually beneficial relationships. Treat conflicts as chances for growth, welcoming constructive feedback to refine your methods and better serve clients and stakeholders. By openly addressing challenges, you foster adaptability and resilience within partnerships, strengthening bonds and positioning relationships for success in ever-changing circumstances, ultimately leading to shared success and enduring collaboration.

Summary

Building trust and fostering long-term relationships is a critical aspect of global selling. By prioritizing trust, practicing transparency, and nurturing relationships, you can establish a strong foundation for success in the international marketplace. Consistency, open communication, cultural understanding, and value creation are key elements in building and maintaining trust with international clients and stakeholders. It is through the fortification of trust that you can forge lasting partnerships that drive mutual growth and prosperity.

From Laughter to Global Ambition

Story 4

While I know this book has your full attention, I have an exciting addition to make. Can you guess what it is? Yes, it's another inspiring story and an incredible vision of my close friend, Mr. Ajay. So, grab a cup of coffee or chai and continue...

You all must remember Mr. Dinesh, yes, he's the close friend I told you about in his success story.

So, it happened like this: Mr. Dinesh was attending an event, and there he met Mr. Ajay Aggarwal. During their conversation, Dinesh mentioned me and expressed his desire to meet me. He thought I could help him expand his business using frameworks I had, which had not only transformed businesses but also brought Indian and international businessmen onto a global platform, creating a new identity for them. It was an identity of their success, their story, their hard work, and their dreams. Dinesh's words were convincing enough for Ajay Ji to want to meet me.

Dinesh Ji scheduled a meeting between me and Ajay, and the three of us met on the agreed date. I inquired about Ajay's vision, and it turned out that his sole vision was to take "Make In India" global. Upon hearing this, I pledged to make every possible effort to support his vision. We discussed the execution of this vision, and I explained my frameworks to him, offering unique solutions that left him astonished. He had sought perfection from many, but he found that perfection in me. He responded with a saying, "बगल में छोरा शहर में ढढोरा!" (A gem in the neighborhood, a diamond in the city!). Hearing this, the three of us burst into laughter, and that's where the beginning of our mission took place.

Chapter 18

Cultural Diversity in Teams: Embracing Diversity and Leveraging it as a Strength

Introduction

Cultural diversity is now a common feature in teams, especially in today's globalized business landscape. This section delves into the importance of not just acknowledging diversity but harnessing it as a powerful asset. By appreciating the advantages of cultural diversity, cultivating inclusivity, and encouraging productive teamwork, global sellers can tap into the complete potential of diverse teams, leading to greater innovation and success.

18.1 The Power of Cultural Diversity in Teams

Examine fundamental factors for unlocking the potential of cultural diversity in teams:

- **Innovation and Creativity:**

  Innovation and creativity thrive in the embrace of cultural diversity. When individuals from various backgrounds, perspectives, and experiences come together, a rich tapestry of thoughts emerges, igniting innovation, inspiring creativity, and paving the way for novel ideas and inventive solutions to emerge. As a result, organizations that prioritize cultural diversity are better equipped to navigate a rapidly changing global landscape, remaining at the forefront of progress and innovation in their respective industries.

- **Broader Market Insights:**

  This broader market insight goes beyond consumer preferences, encompassing a deep understanding of cultural nuances, market trends, and emerging economies. It enables organizations to identify untapped opportunities and create products and services that appeal to a diverse customer base. Diverse teams can anticipate market shifts, navigate regional regulations, and build meaningful global connections, positioning themselves for success in an interconnected, competitive global marketplace.

- **Improved Decision-Making & Adaptability:**

  Diverse teams make better decisions by bringing in many different perspectives and challenging biases. They also adapt more easily to change and can seize new opportunities because team members from different cultural backgrounds share their knowledge and experiences. This helps organizations deal with complex global challenges and become more resilient. Moreover, when diverse voices are included in decision-making, it creates an inclusive and innovative culture that encourages fresh ideas and creative solutions.

This approach not only improves problem-solving but also boosts employee morale and engagement, making the workplace more dynamic. Overall, organizations that value diversity and inclusion benefit financially and enjoy a more inspired and adaptable workforce.

18.2 Fostering Inclusion and Collaboration

Delve into essential factors for promoting inclusion and collaboration:

- **Promote Inclusivity through Effective Communication:**

  Cultivate an environment that embraces diversity and values every team member, ensuring they feel appreciated and empowered to share their individual viewpoints. Nurture a culture of transparency by proactively addressing biases or stereotypes that could impede inclusiveness. In teams characterized by cultural diversity, effective communication is paramount. Encourage candid conversations, attentive listening, and courteous exchange of ideas. Create a space where team members are at ease expressing themselves and are eager to partake in constructive dialogues.

- **Cross-Cultural Training and Education:**

  By investing in cross-cultural training and education, organizations empower their teams to navigate the complexities of a diverse workplace with confidence. This not only minimizes the potential for cultural misunderstandings but also encourages a climate of mutual respect and appreciation for different perspectives. As a result, team members are better equipped to collaborate seamlessly across cultural boundaries, ultimately leading to enhanced productivity and stronger intercultural relationships within the organization.

- **Team-Building Activities:**

  Arrange team-building activities designed to encourage cross-cultural interactions and nurture relationships. Encourage team members to explore each other's cultures, traditions, and values. This not only enhances teamwork but also promotes a more inclusive and empathetic workplace culture. Team members who gain insights into each other's cultures are better equipped to collaborate effectively, leverage their unique strengths, and collectively contribute to the organization's success. These activities serve as a powerful catalyst for improved cooperation and a richer, more harmonious work environment.

18.3 Leveraging Cultural Diversity as a Strength

Explore key considerations for harnessing cultural diversity as a source of strength:

- **Collaboration and Knowledge Sharing:**

  Promote collaboration among team members by harnessing the wealth of diverse backgrounds and experiences they bring to the table. Cultivate a culture that champions knowledge sharing, encourages the free exchange of ideas, and actively cultivates the cross-pollination of diverse perspectives. This approach not only fuels innovation but also enhances the team's problem-solving capabilities.

- **Assigning Diverse Roles and Responsibilities:**

  To maximize the potential of a culturally diverse team, strategically allocate roles and responsibilities that leverage the individual strengths and expertise of team members from varied cultural backgrounds. Harness their unique skills and perspectives to elevate the overall performance of the team. By doing so, organizations can create a dynamic synergy where each member's contributions are valued, leading to not only improved productivity but also a more enriched and innovative work environment.

- **Mentoring and Coaching:**

  Enhance professional growth and development within your diverse team through the implementation of mentoring and coaching programs. Pair team members from various cultural backgrounds to facilitate cross-cultural learning, mentorship, and the effective transfer of knowledge. Such initiatives not only empower individuals to excel in their roles but also promote a culture of mutual support and inclusivity.

- **Conflict Resolution and Cultural Sensitivity:**

  When dealing with conflicts arising from cultural differences in your team, it's important to tackle them promptly and positively. Offer cultural sensitivity training and tools for conflict resolution to foster understanding and respect among team members. This helps the team handle cultural conflicts effectively, promoting a collaborative and harmonious work environment where everyone can work together respectfully and smoothly.

Summary

Cultural diversity in teams presents a wealth of opportunities for global sellers. By embracing diversity, fostering inclusion, and promoting effective collaboration, organizations can leverage the strengths that cultural diversity brings.

When teams embrace different perspectives, work together harmoniously, and capitalize on their collective knowledge, they unlock the full potential of cultural diversity, driving innovation, and achieving sustainable success in the global marketplace.

Chapter 19

Remote Collaboration: Overcoming Challenges and Optimizing Virtual Teamwork

Introduction

In the digital era of today, remote collaboration has surged in prevalence, empowering global sellers to work together seamlessly across geographic boundaries. However, remote work poses unique challenges that require effective strategies to overcome. Within the confines of this chapter, we not only pinpoint the common challenges but also furnish practical insights to optimize virtual teamwork, elevating productivity and ultimately achieving success.

19.1 The Benefits and Challenges of Remote Collaboration

Delve into essential factors for understanding the pros and cons of remote collaboration:

- **Benefits of Remote Collaboration:**

  Remote collaboration offers numerous advantages, including access to a global talent pool, increased flexibility, cost savings, and improved work-life balance. It empowers teams to harness diverse perspectives and expertise, nurturing an environment that spurs creativity and fuels innovation. Additionally, remote collaboration paves the way for reduced commute times, decreased overhead costs, and a reduced carbon footprint, aligning with the evolving dynamics of the modern workforce and the sustainability goals of organizations.

- **Challenges of Remote Collaboration:**

  However, remote collaboration does not come out without its share of challenges, which, if not addressed, can hinder teamwork and productivity. These challenges encompass communication barriers, lack of face-to-face interaction, the potential for misalignment, time zone differences, and the need for effective project management in a virtual environment. It's crucial for organizations to recognize and proactively tackle these obstacles to ensure that remote collaboration continues to be a productive and beneficial mode of working in our increasingly interconnected world.

19.2 Strategies for Overcoming Challenges in Remote Collaboration

Explore crucial elements in crafting strategies to address challenges in remote collaboration:

- **The Art of Effective Communication:**

  Establish clear and consistent communication channels to ensure effective information sharing and collaboration. Utilize a combination of video conferencing, instant messaging, and project management tools to facilitate real-time communication and maintain team connectivity. By adopting these practices, organizations can not only overcome the hurdles of remote collaboration but also harness its full potential, reaping the benefits of a globalized, flexible, and efficient workforce.

- **Building Trust and Connection:**

  Proactively nurturing trust and connection among remote team members is paramount to the success of remote collaboration. To achieve this, it's essential to encourage open and transparent communication channels where team members feel comfortable sharing their thoughts and concerns. Additionally, promoting virtual team-building activities can help bridge the geographical gaps, fostering a sense of unity and shared purpose among team members.

  These informal moments create a more relaxed and humanizing environment, allowing team members to get to know each other on a personal level beyond work-related discussions.

- **Establishing Clear Goals and Expectations:**

  In remote collaboration, clear goals and expectations act as a guiding force for the team's success. It starts with articulating project goals and defining desired outcomes, giving everyone a shared sense of purpose and direction. This shared understanding forms the foundation for effective collaboration. This shared understanding is the foundation upon which effective collaboration is built.

  Additionally, it's crucial to go beyond setting overarching goals and objectives. Clearly defining roles and responsibilities within the team is equally vital. Assigning specific tasks and delineating who is responsible for each task not only streamlines the collaborative process but also fosters accountability. When team members know their roles, they can focus on their responsibilities, reducing the chances of overlapping efforts or gaps in the workflow. This level of clarity minimizes the potential for misunderstandings or conflicts that can arise from ambiguity regarding job responsibilities, ultimately leading to a more harmonious and efficient work environment.

- **Embracing Technology and Collaboration Tools:**

  Harness the power of technology and remote collaboration tools tailored for the virtual workspace. Make the most of project management platforms, file-sharing systems, and virtual whiteboards to boost collaboration, simplify processes, and promote effective teamwork in remote settings. By embracing these digital solutions, organizations can optimize their remote work capabilities and achieve greater productivity and agility.

19.3 Optimizing Virtual Teamwork

Examine essential components for enhancing virtual team performance:

- **Virtual Team Engagement and Motivation:**

  Elevate virtual team engagement and motivation through strategic initiatives. Cultivate a positive work atmosphere by fostering a culture of appreciation and recognition. Celebrate achievements, both big and small, to boost team morale. Additionally, providing regular feedback and opportunities for professional growth not only empowers team members but also strengthens the bond within the virtual team, ensuring a collaborative and motivated remote workforce.

- **Establishing Effective Team Processes:**

  Establish well-defined team processes and protocols tailored for remote collaboration. Create guidelines for managing tasks, making decisions, and resolving conflicts, ensuring a seamless workflow and productive coordination among team members. These structured processes serve as a roadmap for efficient remote teamwork, promoting clarity, accountability, and effective collaboration.

- **Encouraging Autonomy and Flexibility:**

  Grant team members a certain level of autonomy and flexibility in their work. Encourage them to adapt their schedules and work styles to suit diverse time zones and individual preferences, cultivating a strong sense of ownership and empowerment among the team. This autonomy allows team members to optimize their productivity and strike a healthier work-life balance, ultimately contributing to a more motivated and resilient remote workforce.

- **Continuous Learning and Improvement:**

  Cultivate an environment in your virtual team that embraces continuous learning and improvement. Offer avenues for professional development, encourage knowledge sharing, and promote cross-training to elevate skills, enhance collaboration, and keep the team well-informed about industry trends and best practices. By prioritizing continuous learning, not only does the team stay ahead in a rapidly evolving landscape, but team members also feel more engaged and invested in their own growth, contributing to the overall success of the virtual team.

Summary

Remote collaboration presents unique challenges but also offers significant opportunities for global sellers to harness the power of virtual teamwork. By implementing effective communication strategies, fostering trust and connection, utilizing appropriate technology and collaboration tools, and optimizing virtual teamwork processes, organizations can overcome challenges and unlock the full potential of remote collaboration. With an open embrace of remote collaboration, global sellers can achieve increased productivity, foster innovation, and drive success in the global marketplace. - Leadership in a global context: Inspiring and motivating a diverse workforce towards shared goals.

Chapter 20

Staying Ahead of Trends: Monitoring Market Shifts and Adapting Your Strategies Accordingly

Introduction

In today's dynamic business landscape, staying ahead of trends is essential for global sellers to remain competitive and seize new opportunities. Within this chapter, we plunge into the importance of monitoring market shifts, understanding emerging trends, and adapting strategies accordingly. By embracing a proactive approach to trend analysis and strategic adaptation, businesses can position themselves for success in the ever-changing global marketplace.

20.1 The Significance of Monitoring Market Shifts

Probe into the crucial factors of realizing the significance of monitoring market shifts:

- **Anticipating Customer Needs and Identifying Competitive Advantages:**

  Global sellers benefit from monitoring market shifts, enabling them to anticipate evolving customer needs and preferences while staying attuned to changing consumer behavior and emerging demands. Simultaneously, by tracking industry developments, competitor strategies, and disruptive innovations, businesses can identify potential gaps in the market and capitalize on unique opportunities to gain a competitive advantage, aligning their offerings with customer expectations and staying ahead in a rapidly evolving landscape.

- **Expanding into New Markets:**

  Market shifts often present opportunities for geographic expansion. By keeping a pulse on global market dynamics, economic trends, and cultural shifts, businesses can identify untapped markets, assess their potential, and strategically expand their operational boundaries. This proactive approach allows organizations to diversify their customer base, reduce dependency on specific regions, and unlock new revenue streams, all while leveraging their competitive advantages identified through vigilant market monitoring.

- **Mitigating Risks and Challenges:**

  Keeping a close eye on market shifts enables businesses to foresee and proactively address potential risks and challenges. Staying updated on regulatory changes, geopolitical shifts, and technological advancements empowers organizations to adjust their strategies, effectively navigate obstacles, and maintain uninterrupted operations. These strategies not only protect the business but also makes it more resilient in the face of unexpected events. By regularly studying market trends and adapting quickly, companies can navigate uncertain times more effectively, becoming stronger, better prepared, and ready to seize opportunities and overcome challenges in the future.

20.2 Strategies for Monitoring and Adapting to Market Shifts

Explore the approaches to monitor and adjust to market changes:

- **Market Research and Trend Analysis:**

  Dedicate resources to thorough market research, gathering essential data and insights. Employ a mix of primary and secondary research methods, including customer surveys and industry report analysis. This diligence unveils emerging trends, evolving consumer preferences, and the dynamic nature of the market landscape.

  Implement systematic processes for continuous industry trend monitoring and analysis. Utilize technology tools, subscribe to industry publications, participate in conferences, and foster professional networks to stay up-to-date with the latest developments and shifts in your field.

- **Collaborative Partnerships:**

  Forge strategic partnerships with industry experts, consultants, and research firms to gain access to their specialized knowledge and insights. These collaborative partnerships can provide valuable perspectives, data, and expertise to help you navigate market shifts effectively. This not only enhances your understanding of market dynamics but also provides you with a competitive edge. These valuable insights can inform your decision-making, helping you adapt swiftly to market shifts and make informed strategic choices. In essence, collaborative partnerships serve as a dynamic resource, reinforcing your ability to thrive in a rapidly changing business environment.

- **Internal Cross-Functional Collaboration:**

  Promote cross-functional collaboration within your organization by fostering open dialogue and knowledge sharing among various teams, departments, and management levels. This approach nurtures a holistic understanding of market shifts and encourages the generation of innovative ideas. It not only enhances the collective intelligence of the organization but also fosters a culture of adaptability and responsiveness, ensuring that the entire team is aligned in addressing market changes and driving sustainable growth.

20.3 Adapting Strategies to Market Shifts

Implement strategies to respond to market shifts:

- **Agility and Flexibility:**

  Foster a corporate culture that values agility and flexibility. Build the capability to promptly adapt to market changes through the adoption of flexible strategies, adjustment of business plans, and resource reallocation, enabling your organization to capitalize on emerging opportunities and effectively tackle evolving challenges.

- **Continuous Innovation & Customer-Centric Approach:**

  Nurture a culture of continuous innovation and customer-centricity to navigate market shifts effectively. Embrace experimentation, encourage creativity, and invest in research and development to adapt your offerings to evolving customer needs. Additionally, prioritize a customer-focused approach by consistently gathering feedback, conducting market tests, and engaging in co-creation initiatives, ensuring your strategies align with changing customer expectations. This dual commitment to innovation and customer-centricity positions your organization to proactively respond to market changes, staying ahead of the curve and delivering value that resonates with your target audience.

- **Strategic Partnerships and Alliances:**

  Engage in strategic collaborations and partnerships to harness external expertise, resources, and capabilities. Join forces with like-minded businesses, startups, or technology leaders to explore new markets, jointly create innovative solutions, and maintain a leading position amid evolving market dynamics. These alliances not only expand your reach but also provide a collaborative edge in navigating the ever-changing business landscape.

Summary

Staying ahead of trends and effectively adapting strategies to market shifts is a critical aspect of global selling. By proactively monitoring market dynamics, anticipating customer needs, and embracing strategic flexibility, businesses can position themselves as market leaders, capitalize on emerging opportunities, and navigate challenges with resilience. By continuously monitoring, analyzing, and adapting to market shifts, global sellers can maintain their competitive edge and drive sustainable success in the dynamic global marketplace.

Chapter 21

Scaling Your Global Business: Expanding into New Markets and Diversifying Revenue Streams

Introduction

When it comes to growing a global business, there is a need for careful planning to enter new markets and broaden revenue streams. This chapter explores the key considerations and best practices for successfully scaling your business internationally. By grasping the details of market expansion and implementing effective revenue diversification strategies, global sellers can achieve sustainable growth and maximize their global potential.

21.1 Assessing Market Potential

Uncover the vital components of evaluating market feasibility:

- **Market Research and Analysis:**

  When considering expanding into new markets, conduct thorough research to find the best opportunities. Look at factors like market size, growth potential, competition, cultural fit, regulations, and what customers prefer. This helps you decide whether entering a new market is a good idea.

- **Target Market Segmentation & Competitive Analysis:**

  Segment your target market based on demographics, location, lifestyle, and behavior. Identify niche segments and untapped markets that align with your business and offer growth potential. This comprehensive approach helps you pinpoint where to direct your efforts for maximum impact. Additionally, analyze your competition in each target market, understand their strengths and weaknesses, spot market gaps, and develop strategies to differentiate your business and position it for success. By combining precise targeting with strategic differentiation, you can enhance your market entry strategy and increase your chances of success.

21.2 Expanding into New Markets

Discover the essential measures to consider prior to entering new marketplaces:

- **Market Entry Strategies & Localization:**

  Select the optimal market entry strategy considering your business goals, available resources, and risk tolerance. Options include direct exporting, licensing, franchising, joint ventures, strategic alliances, and establishing local subsidiaries or offices. To bolster success, undertake localization efforts by tailoring your products, services, and marketing approaches to align with the target market's unique requirements, encompassing culture, language, regulations, and consumer behavior. This adaptability enhances market acceptance and penetration, ensuring a more effective market entry. Additionally, ongoing market analysis and adaptation are essential to staying responsive to evolving market dynamics and maintaining a competitive edge.

- **Distribution and Logistics:**

  Efficient distribution and logistics are pivotal for successful market entry. Begin by establishing robust distribution networks and nurturing relationships with local partners, distributors, and suppliers. This collaborative approach ensures that your products or services reach the target market effectively.

  Furthermore, pay close attention to logistics management, encompassing shipping, warehousing, customs clearance, and final delivery. By fine-tuning these processes, you not only meet customer expectations by ensuring timely delivery but also enhance your operational efficiency.

- **Legal and Regulatory Adherence:**

  Prioritize a thorough understanding and strict adherence to local legal and regulatory mandates. By immersing yourself in import/export regulations, intellectual property rights, tax obligations, and licensing procedures, you not only mitigate the risk of legal issues but also uphold a reputation built on trust and integrity. Maintaining a strong commitment to legal and regulatory compliance is not just a safeguard against potential challenges but also a cornerstone of sustained success and ethical business practices in the new market.

21.3 Diversifying Revenue Streams

Navigate through the strategic measures to monitor and optimize diversified income streams:

- **Product or Service Expansion:**

  Broaden your product or service portfolio to cater to diverse customer segments and fulfill additional market demands. Identify complementary offerings that align with your core business, leveraging your existing capabilities and customer base to enhance market reach and capture new opportunities. By strategically expanding your product or service offerings, you not only meet evolving customer needs but also strengthen your competitive position and foster sustainable growth in the target market.

- **Geographic Expansion:**

  Consider growing your business by entering regions you haven't explored before. Look for places where you haven't been present yet. Study the market to see if it has potential, adjust your business approach to fit local conditions, and build a reliable network of distribution channels and partnerships in those regions. This helps you reach new customers and markets with ease.

- **E-commerce and Digital Channels:**

  Embrace the online realm as a crucial avenue for your business. Establish a strong internet presence to tap into a broader customer base and unlock additional revenue streams. Develop a robust online platform, ensuring your website is user-friendly for global audiences. Utilize digital marketing tools to enhance customer acquisition and boost sales. By harnessing the power of e-commerce and digital channels, you not only extend your reach but also open doors to significant growth opportunities in the digital landscape.

21.4 Managing Risks and Challenges

Navigate the strategic pathways to effectively managing risks and overcoming challenges:

- **Risk Assessment and Mitigation:**

  Before venturing into new markets or diversifying revenue streams, conduct a thorough risk assessment. Identify potential risks such as regulatory changes, currency fluctuations, cultural barriers, and competitive challenges, and develop contingency plans to mitigate those risks. This proactive approach not only safeguards your business but also enhances its resilience, enabling it to navigate unforeseen circumstances and maintain operational continuity, fostering long-term success and adaptability.

- **Financial Planning and Resource Allocation:**

  In addition to risk assessment and mitigation, effective financial planning and resource allocation are essential for successful expansion and diversification. Evaluate the financial feasibility of new ventures, take into account the potential requirement for additional capital or investment, and strategically allocate resources to support your growth objectives. This meticulous approach not only strengthens your financial footing but also positions your business for sustainable expansion and diversification while minimizing potential financial hurdles.

- **Talent Acquisition and Development:**

  To ensure the success of international expansion and revenue diversification efforts, it's crucial to assemble a diverse and highly skilled workforce. Recruit individuals who possess global expertise, cultural competence, and language skills, as they can be instrumental in navigating new markets. Additionally, invest in ongoing training and development opportunities to continually enhance the capabilities of your employees, ensuring they remain well-prepared to contribute to your business's growth and success in diverse markets.

Summary

Scaling a global business requires a deliberate and strategic approach to expanding into new markets and diversifying revenue streams. By conducting thorough market research, developing localization strategies, establishing strong partnerships, and effectively managing risks, global sellers can successfully navigate the complexities of scaling their business internationally. With careful planning, execution, and a focus on continuous innovation, businesses can achieve sustainable growth, broaden their global footprint, and capitalize on new revenue opportunities.

Chapter 22

Embracing Innovation: Harnessing Emerging Technologies to Drive Global Success

Introduction

Innovation is a key driver of global success, and harnessing emerging technologies is crucial for businesses aiming to stay competitive in the rapidly evolving global marketplace. This chapter explores the importance of embracing innovation and leveraging emerging technologies to propel global growth. By understanding the potential of these new technologies and integrating them into business strategies, global sellers can unlock new opportunities, enhance efficiency, and deliver exceptional value to customers.

22.1 The Role of Innovation in Global Success

Unlocking the path to harnessing innovation for global success in a competitive marketplace:

- **Competitive Advantage:**

  Innovation serves as a potent competitive advantage on the global stage. Embracing cutting-edge technologies allows companies to distinguish themselves from competitors, introduce one-of-a-kind offerings, and secure market share by delivering superior products, services, or customer experiences. Staying at the forefront of innovation is essential to maintaining a competitive edge in the international landscape.

- **Adaptability and Resilience:**

  Innovative businesses are not only more competitive but also better equipped to adapt to market fluctuations and disruptions. By staying at the forefront of technological advancements, businesses can respond quickly to changes in customer preferences, industry trends, and competitive dynamics, ensuring their long-term viability and resilience. The ability to pivot and evolve in response to shifting circumstances is a hallmark of innovative organizations, allowing them to thrive in a constantly changing global landscape.

- **Efficiency and Productivity:**

  Innovation is a catalyst for enhanced operational efficiency and productivity. Emerging technologies have the potential to streamline processes, automate tasks, and optimize workflows, resulting in cost reduction and the liberation of resources. These resources can then be redirected toward value-adding activities and strategic initiatives, further reinforcing the business's competitive advantage in the global landscape.

- **Customer-Centricity:**

  Innovation is a key enabler for businesses to align more closely with customer needs and expectations. By harnessing new technologies, businesses can collect valuable customer insights, tailor offerings, and provide seamless and convenient experiences, ultimately fostering customer loyalty and driving repeat business. This customer-centric approach not only strengthens their market position but also enhances their global competitiveness, ensuring sustainable growth in an ever-evolving business landscape.

22.2 Emerging Technologies for Global Success

Delve into a selection of emerging technologies that hold great promise for global success.

- **Artificial Intelligence (AI) and Machine Learning (ML):**

  Artificial Intelligence (AI) and Machine Learning (ML) technologies are catalysts for business transformation. They empower enterprises to streamline operations, elevate data scrutiny capabilities, and tailor customer engagements, resulting in enhanced efficiency and customer satisfaction. These applications encompass predictive analytics, chatbots, recommendation engines, and demand forecasting, furnishing invaluable insights that bolster the quality of decision-making, optimize resource allocation, and drive innovation. In essence, AI and ML are reshaping the modern business landscape by enabling data-driven strategies and fostering agility in an ever-evolving marketplace.

- **Internet of Things (IoT) & Blockchain:**

  The convergence of Internet of Things (IoT) and blockchain technologies is revolutionizing the business landscape. IoT seamlessly interconnects devices, facilitating data exchange that leads to improved operational efficiency, real-time monitoring, and predictive maintenance. Meanwhile, blockchain ensures transparency, security, and traceability in global transactions. Together, these technologies empower businesses to optimize supply chain management, track inventory in real-time, enable secure cross-border payments, and facilitate smart contracts, all of which foster trust and reduce inefficiencies in global business transactions while enhancing customer experiences through interconnected products.

- **Augmented Reality (AR) and Virtual Reality (VR):**

  Augmented Reality (AR) and Virtual Reality (VR) make customer experiences more fun and engaging. These technologies let companies create exciting virtual product displays, offer immersive virtual tours, and enable teams to collaborate seamlessly across distances. By using AR and VR, businesses not only break down geographical barriers but also tap into new creative ways to captivate customers and deliver exceptional value.

22.3 Integrating Innovation into Business Strategies

See how adding innovation to business can make the market grow even bigger:

- **Nurturing an Innovation-Driven Culture:**

  Cultivate a workplace atmosphere that wholeheartedly welcomes innovation. Inspire employees, regardless of their roles, to engage in imaginative thinking, experimentation, and the enthusiastic sharing of ideas. Create well-defined procedures for generating ideas, conducting thorough assessments, and executing innovations efficiently, granting employees the autonomy to play a significant role in advancing innovative endeavors.

- **Collaboration and Partnerships:**

  Engage in partnerships with technology experts, startups, and research institutions to harness their knowledge and tap into the latest technological advancements. Consider forming strategic alliances that focus on collaborative product development, innovation hubs, or technology incubation, aiming to propel innovation forward and expedite the uptake of innovative solutions.

- **Continuous Learning and Adaptation:**

  Staying informed about new technologies, industry trends, and market shifts is essential for business success. Investing in continuous learning initiatives, training programs, and workshops not only equips your employees with the skills and knowledge they need but also fosters a culture of adaptability and innovation within your organization. This proactive approach ensures your business remains competitive, resilient, and poised for growth in an ever-evolving landscape.

- **Fostering Experimentation and Continuous Improvement:**

  Promote a culture of experimentation and ongoing refinement in the innovation journey. Embrace a mindset that values the lessons learned from failures, encouraging rapid prototyping, testing, and feedback loops to continuously enhance and perfect innovative solutions. This iterative approach not only fuels innovation but also ensures that your organization remains agile and responsive to changing market dynamics, ultimately driving sustainable growth.

Summary

Embracing innovation and harnessing emerging technologies are essential for global success. By incorporating innovative thinking into business strategies, leveraging technologies like AI, IoT, blockchain, AR, and VR, and cultivating a culture of innovation, global sellers can unlock new opportunities, enhance operational efficiency, and deliver exceptional value to customers. Innovation is the driving force behind sustained growth, market leadership, and the ability to thrive in an increasingly dynamic and competitive global landscape.

Author's Remark

Congratulations! You've embarked on an incredible journey to become a global selling expert. With the tips and advice in this book, you're ready to succeed worldwide. Remember, you can sell anywhere—so go out there, do your thing, and become a global selling star! This book is your guide to conquering the world of global sales and achieving success on a grand scale.

In this book, we've covered lots of stuff about being a global seller and finding global success. We talked about things like the good and not-so-good parts of selling globally, dealing with different cultures, finding opportunities around the world, checking out your competition, understanding customers, telling cool stories about your brand, making ads that fit different places, using the internet, sorting out deliveries, finding the right friends to help you sell, and loads more. You're all set for global success!

One cool thing we've learned on this journey is that global selling isn't just about selling in new places; it's a way of thinking that needs you to be flexible, adaptable, and understand different cultures and markets. It means being open to change, trying new things, and grabbing opportunities in a world that's always changing. In this book, we've seen how awesome stuff like technology, including things like AI, the Internet of Things, and more, can make a big difference in how businesses work and connect with customers all around the world. So, remember, staying open to new ideas and using cool tech can help you succeed in the fast-paced global market. It's like having a secret weapon for global success!

As we conclude this journey, we've learned that global success hinges on more than market knowledge. It thrives on trust, cultural understanding, and effective cross-cultural communication. This book has taught us that continuous learning, adaptability, and innovation are essential for sustainable growth. Staying ahead, monitoring trends, and evolving strategies make us industry leaders.

As we wrap up this journey, we've realized that global success requires more than just market knowledge. It hinges on trust, cultural understanding, and effective cross-cultural communication. This book has emphasized continuous learning, adaptability, and innovation for sustainable growth, enabling us to stay ahead and become industry leaders. Armed with these insights, let's embark on our global selling journey with confidence, embrace change, and seize the vast opportunities in the global marketplace. Together, we can shape the future of global commerce and turn borders into gateways to endless possibilities.

Call To Action

Congratulations! on completing the book and gaining valuable insights regarding the global market! Now, you have two choices to elevate your business to new heights:

Option 1: Take the Lead

Armed with the strategies and knowledge from this book, you can step into the driver's seat and implement these techniques in your business. Put your learnings into action and pave your way to success!

Option 2: Personalized Guidance

Interested in personalized guidance and support to ensure you take the right steps towards growth? Schedule a one-to-one meeting with Amar Khurana, the author of this book. Together, we will tailor the strategies to your specific needs, address challenges, and create a roadmap to excellence.

Remember, the journey to success continues beyond these pages. Whether you choose to implement on your own or seek Amar's expertise, you're taking steps towards elevating your road construction business. So, are you ready to make your mark in the Global Industry? Make your choice and let's embark on the road to success together!

To schedule your one-to-one meeting with Amar and kickstart your journey to growth, visit md@inextlogistics.com. Let's make your business thrive!

www.ingramcontent.com/pod-product-compliance
Ingram Content Group UK Ltd.
Pitfield, Milton Keynes, MK11 3LW, UK
UKHW021700190726
13853UKWH00001B/375

9 789355 547484